"Lord, what's in this for You?"

To Harold Hill, that's the number one question that separates the King's kids from the pagans in any situation. In yet another series of King's kid adventures, Hill uncovers the hidden spiritual surprises that await every believer whose reactions are conditioned by "The Manufacturer's Handbook" and whose mouthpiece is programmed for praise. Tucked inside each hilarious episode is a wealth of solid, scriptural truth for you to apply to your own circumstances, whatever they may be. Join Harold Hill in learning the secret of attitude control — adopting the BE-attitudes of the Bible — and watch even the most precarious predicament become a "count it all joy" kingdom opportunity.

Best-selling Harold Hill titles:

Harold Hill
with Irene
Burk Harrell

HOW TO LIVE THE BIBLE

like a king's kid

Power
Books

Fleming H. Revell Company
Old Tappan, New Jersey

Library of Congress Cataloging in Publication Data
Hill, Harold, date
  How to live the Bible like a king's kid.
  (Power books)
  1. Hill, Harold, date 2. Christian biography—United States. 3. Christian life—1960-
I. Harrell, Irene Burk, joint author. II. Title. BR1725.H47A34
269'.2'0924 [B] 80-21782 ISBN 0-8007-5051-9

to
all my readers
who are eager to do
the Bible Thing about *everything*!

Contents

HOW TO LIVE THE BIBLE
like a king's kid

1

How This Book Began

It all started one night in September 1977 when one of the members of our prayer fellowship showed up at our weekly meeting, carrying a problem.

"I've been having trouble sleeping," Jack said. "About three o'clock every morning, I wake up uneasy, so depressed I have to lift up my eyes to see the bottoms of worm holes, and I can't go back to sleep for hours."

He was looking really haggard, as if it would take at least half a dozen sturdy redcaps to carry the black bags under his eyes. All that extra luggage didn't seem to be heaven's best for Jack, so we sat him down in the prayer chair in the middle of the room, gathered round, laid hands on him, and prayed that the Lord would give His beloved sleep.

Our prayer was based on the scriptural promise plainly given in Psalms 127:2: ". . . he giveth his beloved sleep"; so we knew our

prayer was in line with God's will and that He heard us and had
already given us what we asked.

That assurance involved another Scripture, the one in 1 John
5:14, 15, which said, "And this is the confidence that we have in him,
that, if we ask any thing according to his will, he heareth us: And if we
know that he hear us, whatsoever we ask, we know that we have the
petitions that we desired of him."

We were on solid ground, too, in being confident that our prayer
would be answered above all we could ask or think. Bible for that one
was in Ephesians 3:20. The last time I looked, that Scripture read,
"Now unto him that is able to do exceeding abundantly above all that
we ask or think, according to the power that worketh in us."

In every one of our prayers that day, we operated with the
attitude that God's Word was true and that it would work if we did
what it said.

The next week, our formerly sleepless brother walked into the
meeting with a new spring in his step and nothing more than a little
load of carry-on baggage under his eyes. We all praised the Lord for
the good work He had begun to do in Jack, knowing that He would
finish it. We had God's Word for that in Philippians 1:6: "Being
confident of this very thing, that he which hath begun a good work in
you will perform it until the day of Jesus Christ."

After we had rejoiced and praised the Lord for Jack's longer
shut-eye, his testimony went something like this: "Yes, thanks be to
God, my sleep has improved considerably. But I woke up too early
again this morning, with some kind of funny word going through my
mind, a word I'd never heard of. I'm not all that smart, but I even saw
how to spell it: i-n-c-u-b-u-s.

"It seemed important somehow," he explained, "but I didn't
know what it meant, so I telephoned my sister who is a Catholic nun
up in New York State. She didn't know what the word meant, either,
but she told me she'd consult the Mother Superior, who knows
almost everything."

Well, the Mother Superior dug around in the dusty books in the
convent library and found that, among other things, *incubus* is a spirit

of heaviness that comes on people in their sleep and disturbs their rest.

"What do you suppose this is all about?" Jack asked us.

We didn't know exactly, but we did know that *whatever* it was about, God would work it for good for the ones who loved Him and were called according to His purpose.

No matter what comes up in the prayer group, or anywhere else, we stay excited, *knowing* that God's promise in Romans 8:28 is always coming true in our midst: "And we know that all things work together for good to them that love God, to them who are the called according to his purpose."

That night, someone in the fellowship had a revelation from God that we were supposed to call the unwelcome spirit by name and deal with it so our brother would be able to keep sawing logs every morning until the Lord wanted him awake.

Since Mark 16:17 says that one of the signs that would follow believers was that they would cast out demonic spirits in the name of Jesus, we got our attitudes in agreement that God meant what He said in that Scripture and proceeded to put it into action. We collected around our brother again, laid hands on him, and commanded the spirit of incubus to get lost and to keep his icky hands off God's property.

Naturally, since we believed, the Lord moved to perform what His Word promised. Mark 11:24 (NIV) says that's how God works: "Therefore I tell you, whatever you ask for in prayer, believe that you have received it, and it will be yours."

Of course, Jack's snoozing got better and better. All that was pretty wonderful for Jack, and in the meantime the Lord impressed me to ask Him the bottom-line question that had become uppermost in my mind about the whole business: "Lord, what's in this for You?" I knew when I found out what was in it for Him, we'd all benefit. I didn't know then that it was going to turn out to be one of the most significant questions of my life.

2

Chickens and Eggs

Before long, the Lord directed me to look up the roots and branches of the word *incubus* in the dictionary and to move on from there to investigate the word *incubate*. One meaning of *incubate* was "to provide the atmosphere conducive to the hatching out of a living organism from an embryo." That definition wasn't news to me, since I'd grown up on a farm where I'd had plenty of opportunities to watch an old mother hen keep a nestful of eggs warm until the yucky insides had turned into little biddies ready to peck their shells open and get lungs full of fresh air. I knew the mother hen didn't *make* it happen, but she provided the environment where it *did* happen.

Somehow I didn't think the Lord Jesus was instructing me to go into the chicken business and start a feather factory or anything like that. So I read on.

The next definition of *incubate* grabbed me: "to brood, to concentrate on something, to cause to develop, to give form and substance to."

We were out of the egg realm and into the idea realm. *Very* interesting.

I already knew, from having experienced the miseries for myself, what happened when I brooded on a personal injury or resentment. Such incubation was always an invitation for arthritis to hatch out, and it usually did. And when I brooded on a headache, I could magnify it, in nothing flat, from a slight cranial discomfort into a gargantuan pain above the neck.

On the other hand, when I brooded on something good—like a deep-dish apple pie, all weighted down with slabs of cheddar cheese or scoops of cold white stuff—the first thing I knew, I'd arrange to get hold of a hunk of pie, and I'd be sitting before it, fork in hand, trying it on my tastebuds.

It was almost as if brooding on a thing—good or bad—concentrating on it, believing God for it, maintaining the attitude that it *would* happen, had something to do with bringing it into existence and reality in the first place!

Hmmm! Could that be true?

Right away a whole flock of confirming Scriptures flew up from my gizzard, where I had stashed them by meditating on the Word day and night, just as God recommends in Psalm 1.

For instance?

". . .According to your faith be it unto you" (Matthew 9:29). When Jesus said that to blind men who mixed His Word with faith that He could heal them, they received their sight. In other words, when their attitude was that Jesus would enable them to see, it happened. Glory!

Another confirming Scripture was: "If thou canst believe, all things are possible to him that believeth" (Mark 9:23). When Jesus said that to the believing father of a demon-possessed boy, the boy was set free.

Then there was Hebrews 11:1: "Now faith is the substance of things hoped for, the evidence of things not seen." That Scripture had always sounded halfway mysterious to me, before, but it didn't sound mysterious anymore. I realized it was *literally* true. If I had faith that something would come to pass—faith that came as a gift of God (Ephesians 2:8) when I really *heard* and concentrated on some promise in His Word (Romans 10:17)—then my faith, brooding on that promise, would hatch it out! In everyday, nontheological terms, *faith* was my attitude agreeing with God's attitude.

Faith was the *sub-stance*, the underlying foundation, of what I hoped for. My attitude toward God's Word would bring God's Word to pass. What was invisible to start with would become visible!

The potential was there all along in God's promise—just as everything to make the chicken was present in the egg; but faith—a right attitude—like incubation or brooding, was necessary to make it happen.

"Yea, the kingdom of heaven is like unto an unhatched hen's egg," the Spirit seemed to agree. Right away I suspected He was about to teach me another facet of the brooding business, because He's always teaching me things in terms of parables that even an egghead like me can understand.

As I waited before Him, He brought to my remembrance certain truths I had observed as a boy growing up in the country. The first point that registered with me is that you can't hurry a hen. And a hen doesn't try to hurry herself when she's setting a bunch of eggs. She just sits there and lets it happen in the fullness of time, which happens to be twenty-one days.

Every once in a while, she'll put her head down where the eggs are and move it back and forth. As a little boy, I used to think she had gotten the mad itch from sitting so long without getting enough exercise, but my dad told me that wasn't it.

"She's turning the eggs," he explained, "so they'll all get properly exposed to her body temperature. And after a while, it'll be time for things to start happening like popcorn."

I wondered how a hen would know when the time was up—there was no calendar in the hen house—but she always seemed to know. For a while, I kept track, thinking that some hen would get impatient after a couple of weeks and decide to crack the shells herself. I could almost hear her cackle, "Okay, eggs. You've had enough attention from me. I've given you all I've got for two whole weeks now. It's time to get on with it!"

But no hen ever gave up too soon or took things into her own hands and turned a nest of chicks-in-the-making into a scrambled-egg catastrophe. Each always waited patiently, apparently supremely confident, her attitude being that fluffy yellow chicks would happen in the fullness of time if she'd be faithful to do her part and keep the eggs properly cuddled—incubated, that is—according to God's program.

"In the same way," the Spirit seemed to say, "God's promises to the kids of His Kingdom are fulfilled when King's kids are faithful to do their part—brooding patiently, like a mother hen, until heaven's best is born in the fullness of time. But if they get impatient, with an attitude that tries to make those promises happen according to *their* timetables, they blow the whole thing."

Hens and other creatures are smarter than I have been about these things, I decided. I vividly remember sitting on a stump in the woods one day when I was a boy, watching a newborn wasp struggling to get its shoulders out of the wasp cell where it had hatched into existence. When it seemed to be having a hard time of it, I took pity on the critter and said to myself, *Poor fellow. That cell was too tight in the first place. Whoever designed it must not have expected you to be such a big, husky baby. Here, let me help you.* I took my pocketknife and carefully enlarged the opening of the cell, helping the baby wasp along, I thought. I helped him along all right—to the happy stinging grounds, or wherever good wasps go when they're finished with planet Earth.

That prematurely emerged baby wasp easily pulled himself out of the king-size opening of his cell, flopped around a few times, and then keeled over deader 'n a doornail. The struggle to be born must have been an essential part of the wasp-production process. Without that struggle, which would have strengthened his breathing apparatus, he just couldn't make it in the world. I'd killed him with kindness, proving that ". . . the tender mercies of the wicked are cruel" (Proverbs 12:10).

Lots of times I've jumped in and tried to "help" God make His promises come true ahead of His fullness-of-time schedule. When I've had the attitude that I could help God get on with it, the results have been strictly second-best, and I've learned something: I should never try to hurry God.

Thinking along the lines of what happens in a feather factory, I got another insight. This one made it clear why a double-minded man—a man with split-head attitudes—can't expect to receive anything from God (James 1:6–8). Part of the time, the double-minded man is sitting on the right nest, brooding on the good things he desires in line with God's Word, warming up God's promises to the hatching-out stage, but the rest of the time he's putting the good things in cold storage by hopping off that nest, onto another one, incubating the bad things he fears, the things his common sense says he ought to consider.

Double-minded brooding, hopping from one nest to another, switching attitudes from one moment to the next, is continually putting a negative on top of a positive, and they cancel each other out. It works that way in the electrical realm and in the spiritual realm, too. Opposites superimposed short-circuit the promises of God and blow all the fuses. It's like taking a cold, wet blanket of unbelief and smothering everything good that God wants to happen.

"Yes, Hill, without faith it's impossible to please God" (Hebrews 11:6). When the Spirit reminded me of that line from the Bible, it immediately amplified itself in my think tank as, "Hill, if you don't have the right attitude—the attitude that My Word and My ways are the best—you won't ever do anything to suit Me, no matter how hard you try." It sounded pretty conclusive. I understood that when we're full of unbelief, which is like a negative voltage, we effectively block the positive flow of blessings God wants to give us. Negative attitudes are like a logjam, preventing the flow of positive power. That certainty was reinforced by another Scripture that surfaced from another chapter of Hebrews, the one that said:

Let us therefore fear, lest, a promise being left us of
entering into his rest, any of you should seem to come short
of it. For unto us was the gospel preached, as well as unto
them: but the word preached did not profit them, not being
mixed with faith in them that heard it. For we which have
believed do enter into rest. . . . and they to whom it was first
preached entered not in because of unbelief.

Hebrews 4:1–3, 6

That Scripture made it plain that the Israelites' unbelief—their
negative attitude toward God's Word—kept them from the promised
land that God had already prepared for them. He had done His part:
He had prepared the land—but their unbelief kept them from doing
their part: entering in to possess it. Wandering in the wilderness for
forty years was all their fault. A negative attitude had robbed them of
God's best. It'll do it every time. King's kids who want to live in the
promised land learn to stay alert. To coin a new adage: "Your attitudes
will get you if you don't get them first."

In that context, I saw that not only are *we* not pleasing to *God* when
we lack faith—the right attitude toward His Word—*He* can't please
us, either, because only faith—the right attitude—can receive the
pleasing promises of God! The wrong attitude is like a leaky sieve: It
can't hold water. The Scripture backed me up on that insight, where
the letter to the Hebrews recorded: ". . . for he that cometh to God
must believe that he is, and that he is a rewarder of them that
diligently seek him" (Hebrews 11:6).

Terrific, Lord! No wonder it's so important for me and other
King's kids who want heaven's best not to let the garbage of the world
pollute our think tanks. If we do, we foul up the process of
concentrating exclusively on seeking God's Kingdom, because when
we get to thinking about the gruesome things that belong to Slue
Foot's domain of darkness, we forget all about the blessings of God.

It's the old computer principle at work again: GIGO, short for
Garbage In, Garbage Out. If I put garbage in my mind, I can expect to

brood about garbage and be a fertile field for more garbage production, maggots and all. But if I saturate my mind with the promises of God and chew on them continually, just as He recommends, everything good will happen to me.

Think that's too far out? It's exactly what He promises: that if we'll meditate on His Word, having the attitude that His Word is true, we will get excellent results every time. Here's a trio of Scriptures He gave me containing His instructions and guarantees along that line. The first comes at the front end of the Book of Psalms:

> Blessed is the man. . . . [whose] delight is in the law of
> the Lord; and in his law doth he meditate day and night. . .
> he shall be like a tree planted by the rivers of water, that
> bringeth forth his fruit in his season; his leaf also shall not
> wither; and whatsoever he doeth shall prosper.
>
> Psalms 1:1–3

The next verse comes as soon as Joshua gets cranked up:

> This book of the law shall not depart out of thy mouth;
> but thou shalt meditate therein day and night, that thou
> mayest observe to do according to all that is written therein:
> for then thou shalt make thy way prosperous, and then thou
> shalt have good success.
>
> Joshua 1:8

The third Scripture occurs near the beginning of the Proverbs of Solomon, who was the wisest man who ever lived: "My son, forget not my law; but let thine heart keep my commandments; For length of days, and long life, and peace, shall they add to thee" (Proverbs 3:1, 2).

Did I say a trio of instructions and promises? Make that a quartet, to include Jesus saying, "If ye abide in me, and my words abide in you, ye shall ask what ye will, and it shall be done unto you " (John 15:7.)

Looking back over these Scriptures, I saw that they promised prosperity, success, long life, getting what I asked for. . . .

Why, God was clearly saying that if I'd fill my gizzard with the contents of His written Word and keep brooding on them, with the attitude that His Word is true, so many blessings would keep showing up in my life that I'd not be able to find room to put them all!

"That many, Hill?"

"Sure, Lord." My attitude was soaring in the heavenlies by that time. "You said so Yourself, right there in Malachi 3:10: 'Bring ye all the tithes into the storehouse [*I'm more than tithing, Lord*], that there may be meat in mine house, and prove me now herewith, saith the Lord of hosts, if I will not open you the windows of heaven, and pour you out a blessing, that there shall not be room enough to receive it.' "

Hallelujah!

Thinking about the showers of blessing about to pour down from heaven on me, I remembered how Elijah brooded on the sound of an abundance of rain that no one else could hear until the sound became a little cloud no bigger than a man's hand; and as Elijah kept on brooding, he hatched out a genuine goosedrownder that threatened to float away everything that couldn't fly (1 Kings 18:41–45).

Next, the Lord brought to my remembrance the case where Job brought upon himself the very thing he feared (Job 3:25), and the time when. . . .

I could feel my spiritual antennae stretching up to hear all the Lord was going to reveal to me. Talk about being excited! I was! No wonder, because the Lord was opening up a whole new area of Bible study for me, and with it, an expanded King's-kid life-style more full of potential for abundant living than anything I'd ever before experienced!

3

Brooding–From Genesis to Revelation

I first began to experience abundant living when I became a King's kid twenty-five years ago, after forty-eight years of being a devout pagan. As a pagan, I was tangled in all the trappings of what *looked* like abundant life to the world: I was a supersuccessful electrical engineer and inventor, president of my own company, owner of a yacht and a Mercedes-Benz, a proud member of all the most exclusive clubs, a fellow with millions of dollars at my disposal, hobnobbing with the jet set here and abroad. But down inside, where I really lived, I was such a total disaster area that I started trying to drink myself to death with alcohol. When that didn't bring on corpsehood fast enough to suit me, I tried drinking a more concentrated deadly poison, but it didn't stay down.

Suicide was the first thing I had ever failed at in my life. It was a new experience for me. (You can read all the hairy details in my first book, *How to Live Like a King's Kid*.) That failure drove me to my knees one night, where an anguished cry came from my lips: "God, help me!"

Without knowing what I was doing, I was putting into operation one of the promises of God that works every time—the promise concerning which Paul reminded the Romans when he wrote to them: "As the scripture says, 'Everyone who calls out to the Lord for help will be saved'" (Romans 10:13 TEV).

Well, He not only saved me, He helped me, and He keeps on helping me in remarkable ways, many of which are chronicled elsewhere. (Besides the original King's-kid book, there are five more so far, not counting this one, all telling some things about my adventures in eternal life on planet Earth. The books full of adventures have come so thick and fast since I became a King's kid that I've sometimes suspected God was trying to make me a one-man proof of the Scripture that says, ". . . of making many books there is no end . . ." [Ecclesiastes 12:12].)

One of the first things I did after I became born again by trusting Jesus to save me was to examine the contents of the Holy Bible, which I understood to be God's Word in written form. Since it was full of instructions for living and case histories of the good things that happened to folks who followed His instructions—and the calamities that befell those who didn't—I decided to take God's advice about how I was to operate. Right away I gave His leatherbound, gilt-edged instructions a name it would take an egghead engineer to dream up. To me, since God was my Creator and I was His product, the Bible was obviously the Manufacturer's Handbook.

Up to that point in my life, except for goofing suicide, I had succeeded at everything I had ever tried. There was nothing mysterious behind my success rate. I had succeeded for a very simple reason: I had followed directions. Already I had found it to be a reliable principle of life that if I followed directions, I got results, provided the directions were given by somebody who knew what he was talking about.

Since, for forty-eight years, I had studied under the most capable teachers, gotten the best possible education, and applied the knowledge of the best books available to get excellent results in my secular life, when I met Jesus, I said, "I'll do the same thing with the Bible. I'll read the Manufacturer's Handbook and do what it says, so I can enjoy the best my heavenly Father has for me this side of heaven." From the beginning, I adopted the attitude that the Manufacturer's Handbook was reliable and that I could depend on it to perform perfectly, whenever I followed the instructions, just as I had learned to do with appliances and machinery.

People had smiled at me rather indulgently and wagged their heads and said, "You're crazy, Hill. The Bible doesn't work that way."

But I tried it anyway and found out *they* were the ones who were crazy, putting their own minds ahead of God. The Bible *did* work that way, and its been working that way ever since, every time I try it. I simply read it and do it and experience superior results every time. When I don't do it? Woe is me!

One Scripture the Lord laid on me, hard, about the brooding business was Philippians 4:8. You've heard it before, and so had I. I'd even quoted it and recommended it to other people, but I'd never quite seen what He was getting at the way I saw it the day He got me to brooding about the incubation process. The Scripture goes like this:

Finally, brethren, whatsoever things are true, whatsoever things are honest, whatsoever things are just, whatsoever things are pure, whatsoever things are lovely, whatsoever things are of good report; if there be any virtue, and if there be any praise, think on these things.

Chances are, God wasn't telling me to think about good things just as an interesting mental exercise. I knew He meant to *accomplish* something if I'd be obedient to brood according to His instructions. If I'd do my part, He'd bring the good things into manifestation!

I'd thought about good things often, and I'd even experienced the peace He talked about in the verses before and after this one, but now I was being increasingly persuaded that thinking about good things, brooding on them, incubating them in my think tank, was actually part of the process He had designed to bring the good things into being!

It was a real mindblower, and I knew I'd have to check it out systematically and thoroughly in other parts of the Scripture to make sure it lined up with them.

Do you know what I discovered? The brooding concept was verified right there in the very first chapter of Genesis, where, in the beginning, "the Spirit of God was *brooding* upon the face of the water" to bring forth all creation from what was invisible to start with! (Hebrews 11:3 LB). (See variorum reading in *The Logos International Study Bible* at Genesis 1:2. In further confirmation of the brooding principle, a leading commentary makes this startling statement: "The chaos has underlying it the idea of a cosmic egg which was hatched by the brooding Spirit, as by a bird, to produce the universe . . ."[*The Interpreter's Bible*, vol. 1, p. 466].)

If brooding was there in what God had Moses write down in the beginning of the Manufacturer's Handbook, I wanted to see if it was in the end, too, so I skipped over the whole middle section, for the time being, to check the last two chapters of God's revelation to John. Again, jackpot! When John started describing the new heaven and the new earth (Revelation 21:1), I got so all caught up with him in brooding about the wonderful things being shown him by the Spirit of God, that by the time he got around to saying, ". . . Even so, come Lord Jesus" (Revelation 22:20), I was saying it, too, centering all my thoughts on Him, expecting Him to float down from the clouds any minute (Acts 1:11).

There isn't a King's kid alive who can read those passages and not start brooding on the Alpha and Omega, the Author and Finisher of our faith (Hebrews 12:2), the One we find when we seek Him with all our hearts (Jeremiah 29:13). What a feast for brooding that is!

In the following weeks, I found that the truth about brooding wasn't just in the first and last chapter of the Manufacturer's Handbook; it was everywhere in between, in more places than I could count. There was even a neat summary of them almost in the middle of the book: "The fear of the wicked, it shall come upon him: but the desire of the righteous shall be granted" (Proverbs 10:24).

In other words, the wicked man would brood on the things that scared the liver out of him, since he wouldn't be equipped with the perfect love that casts out fear (1 John 4:18); and sure enough, hair-raising horrors would jump out at him in broad daylight. But the righteous man would be continually thinking of the good things of God, and he could walk through the valley of the shadow of death without the first goosebump (Psalms 23:4). It's all a matter of attitude toward God and His Word.

Another Psalm puts it this way: "Delight thyself also in the Lord; and he shall give thee the desires of thine heart" (Psalms 37:4).

For the man with a heart right toward God, good things will continually happen, just as the Scripture promises. Any time I am delighting myself in the Lord, He is planting His own desires for me in my heart. They *have* to come to pass, because they're in line with His perfect will for my life. As I delight in the Lord and brood on the good things He causes me to desire, I'm following His plan to incubate them into reality.

My attitude determines the outcome, every time! I never have to be "under the circumstances," because I can be above them, controlling them. Since I can control my attitude, and my attitude can control the circumstances—*Glory!*

By learning to brood according to His Word, I can become a co-creator with God! Preposterous? Not according to John 14:12, which I'd never gotten a handle on, until now. Just consider it: "Verily, verily, I say unto you, He that believeth on me, the works that I do shall he do also; and greater works than these shall he do; because I go unto my Father." It was true! I'd be doing the same things Jesus was doing, right along with Him. But it wouldn't swell my head, because I knew that: ". . . all that we have accomplished you [God] have done for us" (Isaiah 26:12 NIV).

The brooding principle—God's method for us to incubate His promises into reality—permeated the Bible, and it tied together many concepts the Lord had been teaching me for a long time. More than ever, it made me want to be saturated with the Word of God, so I could brood on it continually and so put myself in a position to experience everything God had to offer for King's-kid living.

Hey! That must have been part of what God had in mind in Isaiah 55:10, 11, where He said:

> For as the rain cometh down, and the snow from heaven, and returneth not thither, but watereth the earth, and maketh it bring forth and bud, that it may give seed to the sower and bread to the eater: So shall my word be that goeth forth out of my mouth: it shall not return unto me void, but it shall accomplish that which I please, and it shall prosper in the thing whereto I sent it.

The Word *works* when we receive it and hold it as the land holds the rain. It brings forth fruit! All that was exciting to know. It was exciting, too, to see how every time the Lord teaches me something new, He takes me back and confirms it by weaving it into harmony with everything else He has already taught me in His Word. This brooding business was no exception.

But I learned right away that it wasn't enough for me to know the theory of it and see how it fit with other things the Lord had taught me. In order to fully experience its blessings, I'd have to see it demonstrated, not only in Elijah accounts in the Bible, but in past, present, and future events in my own life.

At first, learning to live the Bible as far as the brooding principle was concerned was something like learning to ride a bicycle when I was a boy. For a long time before I had a bike of my own, I studied the theory of bike riding by watching other kids in the neighborhood do it.

"I can ride a bike," I told myself, about to burst with the recommended positive attitude. "It's easy. All I have to do is get on and stay vertical. That's all there is to it."

Then came the day when I had an opportunity to put my theoretical knowledge into practice. What happened? Total disaster. I must have gotten on and fallen off seven or eight hundred times before I really got the hang of it.

Now, there was nothing wrong with my theory: It was right-on from the beginning. The problem was, I had the head knowledge, but the body knowledge just wasn't there. And it could come only by painful experience.

For days my trial and error was 100 percent error. My kneecaps still show the scars. We had dirt and gravel roads in those days, and a good part of the paving is still inside my knee joints. Some of the rocks must have been full of iron, because the metal-detecting machinery at airports squeals sometimes when I walk through the archway or the attendant runs the gadget down my legs.

But painful as the learning process was, I wouldn't have given up for anything. I said, "I'm going to ride that thing if it kills me," and it almost did. But I had "come as a little child," and not once was I tempted to chicken out and say, "I'll never get the hang of it." And even when I was holding on for dear life, I kept dreaming of the day when I'd be able to holler, "Look, ma! No hands!"

Sure enough, one day I climbed aboard and sailed away, upright. I had no more knowledge of theory than I had on the days when the ground pulled me down like a magnet, but suddenly my theory worked. And from then until now, I can ride a bicycle. My theory became real in practical experience, and nothing could take it away from me, not even the law of gravity.

I'm trusting that's how it's going to be when I have had enough practice living the Bible along the lines of the brooding principle. As I approach God's Word with a right attitude, it'll start working for me more times than not, instead of the other way around. I'll start consistently acting like someone who has the mind of Christ (1 Corinthians 2:16). Meanwhile, I'm still practicing. Like Paul, I know

I haven't yet reached the goal (Philippians 3:12), but I know I'm headed in the right direction.

I want to tell you some of my experiences in all this, but first, time out for a little instruction for readers who haven't already taken the steps necessary for enjoying all the abundant-life benefits of King's kids in action.

4

King's Kids and the Other Kind

It's very easy to become a fully equipped King's kid in training. Just follow these three simple steps:

1. Be born again, by believing and receiving Jesus and trusting Him to save you. Here's how that's spelled out in the Manufacturer's Handbook:

"But to all who received him, he gave the right to become children of God [that's King's kids!]. All they needed to do was to trust him to save them. All those who believe this are reborn!— not a physical rebirth resulting from human passion or plan—but from the will of God."

John 1:12, 13 LB

2. Invite Him to take over your life as Lord of all of it, knowing that apart from Him, you have nothing to offer. Scripture says it this way:

"And so, dear brothers, I plead with you to give your bodies to

31

God. Let them be a living sacrifice, holy—the kind he can accept. When you think of what he has done for you, is this too much to ask?"

"Don't let the word around you squeeze you into its own mould, but let God re-make you so that your whole attitude of mind is changed. . . ."

"Then you will be able to know the will of God—what is good and is pleasing to him, and is perfect."

Romans 12:1 LB 12:2 PHILLIPS; 12:2 TEV

3. Ask God for His Holy Spirit, who is given to those who believe in Him:

"If ye then, being evil, know how to give gifts unto your children, how much more shall your heavenly Father give the Holy Spirit to them that ask him?"

Luke 11:13

"On the last and greatest day of the Feast, Jesus stood and said in a loud voice, 'If a man is thirsty, let him come to me and drink. Whoever believes in me, as the Scripture has said, streams of living water will flow from within him.' By this he meant the Spirit, whom those who believed in him were later to receive. . . ."

John 7:37–39 NIV

Simple as one, two, three. Once you have taken these steps, you're in line to begin to enjoy the life more abundant (John 10:10), the life of joy (John 16:24), and the life of peace (John 14:27) that he can give us when we follow His instructions, having the attitude that says His way will work. (For further details, read *How to Live Like a King's Kid*, which tells how I got started in Kingdom living.)

Once you've become a King's kid, you can let the Holy Spirit reprogram your think tank to think the thoughts of God instead of the second-best common-sense human alternatives. You can begin to live in heaven as children of God while you're still earthlings ambling around on this planet.

"Absurd!" shouts your Educated Idiot Box, and mine. Didn't you know it would? According to Isaiah 1:5, ". . . the whole head is sick. . . ." That's why it always tries to keep you from God's best by planting negative attitudes. But take it from me, you don't have to pay any attention to your sick head. If you can't take my word for it, try Proverbs 3:5: ". . . lean not unto thine own understanding."

Frankly, our brains are good for little more than getting us into trouble and for keeping our hair out of our eyes, until they're recycled to contain the mind and attitudes of Christ.

Repeatedly, throughout the pages of the Manufacturer's Handbook, the Manufacturer—God—tells the product—us—that the Kingdom of heaven is right here, right now; that we are, in fact, already in heaven if we choose to be. Scriptures? Try on these two for size:

> . . . For behold, the kingdom of God is within you (in your hearts) and among you (surrounding you).
>
> Luke 17:21 AMPLIFIED

> But God, who is rich in mercy, for his great love wherewith he loved us, Even when we were dead in sins, hath quickened us together with Christ, (by grace ye are saved;) And hath raised us up together, and made us sit together in heavenly places in Christ Jesus.
>
> Ephesians 2:4–6

Our failure to enjoy all God has for us, to partake of heavenly living here and now, our propensity for settling for crummy second-best, is well documented throughout the pages of history. But we no longer have to let it be so.

The way out involves dethroning common-sense attitudes, which are based on the evidence of our limited senses and the blown mind of our top ten inches, and latching onto divine-sense attitudes, inheriting the Kingdom, by faith and patience (Hebrews 6:12) brooding into eyeball reality the promises set forth in the Manufacturer's Handbook.

We start out by steeping ourselves in the Word of God so we can *know* His promises and claim them. In the process, He actually plants His mind and attitudes in us (1 Corinthians 2:16). How can that be?

Search me. I don't have to know how it can be; I just have to believe it is, because God says so.

Long ago I learned never to read the Manufacturer's Handbook to find out why or how to argue with God about things. I just read it to see what He recommends, take His Word for it, and then learn all I need to know about how it works by putting it into action.

The life-style of a real King's kid is one that transcends the limitations of our five ordinary senses: seeing, hearing, smelling, tasting, and touch. That equipment is good enough for pagans, because they are still living in the dimensions of one world only. But what is good enough for pagans is not good enough for King's kids. We are equipped with something far better:

1. The mind of Christ (1 Corinthians 2:16) with which to do our thinking
2. The promises of God to think about (Matthew 4:4)
3. The nine gifts of the Holy Spirit (1 Corinthians 12:7–10) to put it all into forward motion

With all this extra equipment, King's kids can expect out-of-the-ordinary results. They find problems turned into adventures as they use the mind of Christ to brood on the promises of God and hatch out God's perfect will in every case, using the gifts of the Spirit to put His will into operation in the affairs of men.

That's quite a bundle! Sound too good to be true? You can give it the acid test: Try it yourself, and look around you.

When disaster threatens, you can always tell the pagans from the King's kids by looking or listening. In the face of what looks like absolute ruin, pagans pale and panic. King's kids grin their glory grins and keep on praising the King for being in charge of His Kingdom to bring good out of everything for Him and for them, no matter how dreadful it looks.

Being in a position of faith and patience to receive special treatment and acting as if they expect the very best to happen all the time is the life-style of King's kids who have learned to live the Bible, brooding on the Word (Psalms 1:2), praising God at all times, thanking Him for everything (Ephesians 5:20), and praying without ceasing

(1 Thessalonians 5:17). And because it is better to give than to receive (Acts 20:35), they have a super fringe benefit: they are able to be His instruments for imparting God's best to others whom they encounter along the way.

Exactly what is the best? you might be wondering. *What does God want for us? What does abundant life, eternal life, heavenly living, include?* Why, it includes everything good: love, joy, peace, righteousness, and perfect health and prosperity. These last two are so plainly stated in John's third letter, to Gaius, that a lot of folks have missed them: "Beloved, I wish above all things ['above *all* things' sounds like a pretty high priority!] that thou mayest prosper and be in health, even as thy soul prospereth" (3 John 2). He goes on to say that he has no greater joy than to hear that God's children are walking in truth (3 John 4). Continuing in that truth—God's Word to His children (John 17:17)—is the avenue to becoming true disciples, Jesus said (John 8:31). And it is His disciples, and only His disciples, who are promised the knowledge of the truth that will set them free (John 8:31, 32). Free from what? Free from all that would bind them. That figures, because His disciples are the only ones interested in reading His Word, knowing His Word, and doing His Word.

This book, then, is a look at the whole matter of brooding on the Word of Truth, living the Bible. Here is the exciting, satisfying, abundant life that multitudes reject in favor of following the dictates of their common sense, but that King's kids embrace as the perfect plan of God.

It is the hope and prayer of this King's kid that this sharing of what I am continuing to learn will enable you to enter more fully into your inheritance as King's kids—a life so much more abundant you'll have to pinch yourself to believe it's real!

And now, on with the attitude adventures!

5

The Case of the Broken Fan Belt

Watching God fulfill His promise contained in Romans 8:28 has long been one of my favorite spare-time occupations: "And we know that all things work together for good to them that love God, to them who are the called according to his purpose."

He's given me plenty of opportunities to brood on the truth of that over the years of my King's-kid life. Take one Saturday afternoon a few months ago, for instance. My friend Dick and I had driven to a town about fifty miles from nowhere, so I could speak at a Full Gospel meeting at the local high school. We had assumed it was an eating meeting; but when we arrived, there were no groceries in sight. "This isn't a dinner meeting," the folks explained when they heard our stomachs growling at each other. "But there's plenty of time. Why don't you drive down the road about four miles to the restaurant and have dinner? We'll crank up a song service in the meantime; and when you get back, the folks will be in gear to hear you speak."

That sounded a whole lot better than having a hungry pity party, so we praised the Lord and did the next thing: went to supper. On the way, I started brooding about how the Lord was working everything for good as we drove down the country road and pulled into the restaurant parking lot.

Before I turned off the ignition, the red light on the dash flashed at me: motor hot. Suspecting a broken fan belt, even though the car had just had its 20,000-mile check up, I raised the hood, confirmed the diagnosis, and praised the Lord that He had added one more ingredient to the recipe He was stirring together for good that night.

At that point, a pagan would have panicked himself into purple apoplexy. How do I know? I've been there. I've seen it happen. If he survived that, he'd have continued to brood up the elements for a full-scale disaster. I can hear him now, like a loud echo from the not-too-distant past: "There we were, fifty miles from nowhere, and all the mechanics had gone to bed with the chickens. Furthermore, they'd never heard of a Mercedes-Benz diesel imported automobile that far out in the sticks, much less stocked a fan belt to fit one. No other cars for miles around, no way we could have gotten back to the meeting place in time without blisters even if we'd headed out hoofing it right that minute—which was out of the question anyhow since our insides were grinding together with emptiness.

"Woe is me!"

In just a few minutes, a dyed-in-the-polyester pagan could have brooded a cataclysmic end of the world out of one little broken fan belt. Given his negative attitude, he'd have been stranded and starved, and he'd have scuttled his speaking engagement and worn holes in his soles groveling his way home down the gravelly road in the dark. With his kind of luck—all "luck" comes from Lucifer, that's why it's always bad—he'd have fallen into the drainage ditch at least twice and gurgled his muddy way to the top, with his pockets full of tadpoles.

But King's kids? Forget it! Negative attitudes are banished from them, since they're containers for Jesus (2 Corinthians 4:7; 13:5), by His grace. So Dick and I magnified the Lord instead of magnifying the dismal prospects and praised our heavenly Daddy for the entire situation, tadpoles and all. He's the One who permitted it, and He's the One who would get us out of it—with more good for us and glory for Him than if it hadn't happened. All we had to do was to praise Him, brood on His unmistakable promise in Romans 8:28, and go inside the restaurant and order the most delicious-sounding meal on the menu.

A few minutes later, while our amens after asking the blessing were still reverberating around the table, Brother Glenn, a King's kid from our church back in Baltimore, just happened to come along with his wife to have dinner.

We momentarily stopped slurping our soup to pass the time of day with them.

"I saw the hood of your car open," Glenn said. "Catching flies? Or are you having trouble?"

"Neither one," I told him. "Hood's open to let the motor cool off. The car happens to have a broken fan belt, but we're doing fine."

I told him about the speaking engagement down the road and how sure I was that the Lord had everything under control and was working it all together for good.

"Well, praise the Lord," he agreed. And right away he volunteered to take over on the automotive front. He said if something good was going to happen, he wanted to be in on it. We couldn't blame him for that. Our part was to continue to praise the Lord, keep brooding on His promise to hatch it out, and enjoy the good country cooking.

I discovered long ago that one of the most important principles of victorious King's-kid living is to refuse to worry about my heavenly Daddy's business, His property, or any of His affairs. As a matter of fact, I've learned that even *I* am none of my business.

"What a cop-out!" you say? It's a mighty good one, saves me the trouble of ulcers, nervous breakdowns, high blood pressure, and exorbitant shrink fees. That's why I go around recommending such an attitude to everybody.

Anyhow, Brother Glenn said, "By a strange coincidence, my father-in-law lives near here in Westminster, and he will know where you can get service and parts—even on a Saturday afternoon."

"Wonderful!" I told him, realizing it wouldn't be that easy unless the King of kings was clearly in charge, doing exceedingly abundantly above all we could ask or think, according to His power at work in us who believe (Ephesians 3:20). If I'd been using my common-sense attitude, I'd have been worrying up a storm. But I was counting on the Word and doing it:

> Be careful for nothing; but in every thing by prayer and supplication with thanksgiving let your requests be made known unto God. And the peace of God, which passeth all understanding, shall keep your hearts and your minds through Christ Jesus.
>
> Philippians 4:6, 7

That Scripture had encouraged me to give my common-sense attitude away to Jesus in exchange for something a whole lot better.

"Lord, I want Your thinking on every subject," I'd told Him, and I could tell He was working on it.

As He set me to thinking, "Lord, what's in this for You?" He kept me from any tendency toward a "poor little ol' me" pity party I might otherwise have thrown when things didn't go exactly according to *my* plans. God has repeatedly shown me that pity parties are the pits. It's a lot more fun to rejoice continually, again and again (1 Thessalonians 5:16), and to keep on praising God all the time. That gets infinitely better results too.

Well, before Dick and I could polish off our dessert, Glenn had come back with his father-in-law, a fan belt, and a whole tool chest full of wrenches, pliers, and screwdrivers. Since there were several adjustments to be made under the hood, Glenn chauffeured us back to the meeting, dropped us off, and returned to the restaurant to make like a mechanic.

"Go ahead and speak as long as they'll let you," he'd told me. "Don't worry about a thing. It's all under control."

I knew that was true, so while the grease monkeys did their thing, I stood before the audience and did mine: I bragged on Jesus. And it wasn't one of my shorter talks, which was a good thing, as it turned out. When I was driven back to the restaurant about midnight, the work on my car wasn't quite finished. It seems the first fan belt had been the wrong size; the tool chest full of hardware had been inadequate; and a second shift of mechanics had had to take over.

Too bad? Not at all.

The Lord must want us to linger here a while longer, I knew, remembering that all things are of God (2 Corinthians 5:18) and wondering what further ingredient He might be planning to add to the good things He was working on for that occasion.

I didn't have to wait long to find out. At that moment, another car wheeled into the parking lot. The driver stuck his head out the window and asked the standard question: "Having trouble?"

"No, no trouble," I explained. "Just a series of King's kids' adventures in progress. And since you're here, you're probably one of the 'all things' the Lord is working together for good tonight."

By that time, the man's wife, who was sitting beside him, had recognized me by my attitude. "Harold Hill!" she shrieked. "Fancy meeting you here! I was going to the high school to hear you speak tonight, but one of our friends had an accident. He was driving a nail when it snapped off and flew right into his eyeball. Looks bad; he's scheduled for immediate surgery. Would you like to pray for him?"

"Is a bluebird blue?" I asked her, knowing God hadn't sent her there for nothing. The next thing I knew, we were having a parking-lot prayer meeting, not just for the friend whose eyeball got nailed, but for the woman's husband, too, who just happened to be the owner of the restaurant. He was having severe breathing problems— sounded like terminal emphysema, at best—so we laid hands on him while we were at it.

The man felt so much better after our prayer that he dug a ringful of keys out of his pocket, unlocked the restaurant, and treated everybody in the parking lot to cold drinks. That's when his wife told me she'd been seeking the baptism in the Holy Spirit, and while I officiated at that ceremony, work on my car got wound up.

When the second shift of mechanics was wiping the grease off their hands, I asked, "Whom do I owe—and how much?" Two shifts of mechanics for five hours couldn't amount to less than a hundred dollars, I knew, to say nothing of the fan belt and other accessories that had to come from someone's pocket.

Nobody seemed to know the answers to my questions. They all just shrugged their shoulders and looked at one another. I put my billfold back in my pocket, praised the Lord, and headed for home, figuring I could stop by at a later date, earlier in the day, and pay the piper.

The next week, I drove back to the restaurant and made inquiry. "What about the bill for fixing my car the other night?" I asked the restaurant owner.

"What *about* the bill?" he asked me.

"Somebody must have paid for labor on my car, and I want to reimburse whoever it was."

"Oh, *that* bill," he said. "It's all taken care of. I just gave the mechanics a few steaks out of the freezer, and everybody went home happy. What's the matter? Aren't *you* happy?"

"I'm delighted—in orbit!" I chortled. "A fellow would have to be a complete idiot to complain about treatment like that. And by the way, I notice you're breathing much better today."

"Sure am," he grinned. "Jesus healed me. And when the surgeon examined the man with the nailed eyeball, ready to sew it up, he couldn't find any hole. Thought it was a case of mistaken identification. Told the nurse she had sent him the wrong patient. The guy didn't match his chart."

My informant slapped his thigh and doubled over in a guffaw that would have been terminal for anyone with imperfect breathing apparatus, and I had a glory party all the way home. Jesus had worked everything for good, just as His Word guaranteed. A bunch of heaven had happened that night, which we'd have missed if it hadn't been for the broken fan belt. It made me glad that the mechanics who had given my car its checkup had goofed, overlooking the fan belt's weakened condition.

Was their oversight an accident? No way, because there are no accidents in the lives of King's kids. Everything that happens to us—or to our vehicles—God permits for a reason.

Did right brooding and attitudes that expected good results play a real role in all this? Or would the good things have taken place even if we'd brooded on the negative instead? Good question! I'm glad I didn't have to experience the answers. As it was, I avoided having to endure anything second-best. Until God tells me otherwise, my plan is to keep on praising Him for everything from now on. Of course, the best-laid plans of mice and men *can* go astray, but He can still come to our rescue even after we have heard His Word but done our own thing.

It's been a lifesaver for me that He never leaves us or forsakes us, even when we're disobedient. Take one afternoon at the Canadian border, for example. That was an adventure that almost landed me behind bars. . . .

6

The Case of the Hot Hitchhiker

Living the Bible of Proverbs 3:5–7 and getting the truth of it cemeted solidly into my gizzard so I'll never stray from it has involved some shaky experiences for me. That Word says:

> Trust in the Lord with all thine heart; and lean not unto thine own understanding. In all thy ways acknowledge him, and he shall direct thy paths. Be not wise in thine own eyes; fear the Lord, and depart from evil.

I've found it easy enough to persuade myself that I was trusting the Lord with all my heart, but sometimes I've found myself with my attitude leaning on my own understanding without realizing what I was doing until it was almost too late. It goes without saying that any time I've *deliberately* leaned on my own understanding, thinking I was sufficiently wise to conduct my own affairs without any guidance from on high, I've lived to regret it.

I'm still not sure exactly what transpired the day I was driving home from Toronto, Canada.

Whenever I'm in that area and approach the region of Niagara Falls, I know I'll get mixed up, because I always do. There are signs pointing to Fort Erie, and because I've never learned where it is in comparison to other places, I invariably take the wrong turn. It's always my fault for having the wrong attitude. It's almost as if I say, "Lord, I'm going to goof it," thereby putting in an order for the wrong thing to take place. Having perfect faith in failure and testifying to it with my lips, I've been dead right about being dead wrong.

You'd think I'd have learned these things, since I've taught them so often, but apparently teachers don't necessarily learn automatically. If they did, Paul wouldn't have bothered to ask, "Thou therefore which teachest another, teachest thou not thyself? . . . (Romans 2:21).

So that I won't mislead you, be sure not to do what I do, but do what the Scripture says you should do. That way, you can't go wrong, even with me in your midst. A man will always go wrong, looking to his own schemes, and that day—God help me—I did.

As I approached the signs that had always confused me, instead of asking God to guide me, I prayed, "Lord, I sure could use a copilot on this trip." Saying amen, I looked up the road and saw a hitchhiker with his thumb stuck out.

"Hallelujah!" I hollered. "Thank You, Lord, for having the copilot standing there before I called. Now, I'll just pick him up, and he'll be able to give me perfect directions, because hitchhikers always know where they're going."

It's as clear to me now as it is to you that I was putting my sick head in charge of the situation. How do I know? I didn't even ask the Lord whether or not I should pick up the fellow. That's a pretty important question for King's kids to ask the Lord these days when all kinds of second-best things are statistically likely to clobber hitchhiker picker-uppers. When our attitudes and actions lean to our own understanding in these things, we risk forfeiting God's protection, but I didn't think about that, at first.

The young man was carrying a huge suitcase, a real albatross. *Kind of unusual for a thumber*, I thought. Generally, they travel light.

Well, he shoved his albatross onto the upholstery in the backseat and thanked me for the lift as he deposited himself in the front seat beside me.

"Where you headed?" I asked him, pulling off the shoulder and starting down the highway.

"To work on my brother's farm in New York State," he said. "Been working on a farm in Ontario."

We talked for a little about other things, and then I got to the real question—the only one that matters: "How long have you known Jesus?"

He gave me the usual string of evasive answers, telling when he was baptized, when he joined the church, how long his parents had sung in the choir. But it finally came down to the point that he didn't really know Jesus yet but he said he was willing to make His acquaintance. We prayed; I handed him a little New Testament from the glove compartment; and we praised the Lord together. But even in the midst of all that , my spirit detected something offbeat about the whole proceeding. He was too enthusiastic, as if he had an ulterior motive.

The Holy Spirit was sounding a little warning bell, but I didn't know yet what it meant. Anyhow, I prayed silently, "Lord, this is Your trip. I've just lifted You up to this young man, and You promised that if we'd lift You up, You'd draw all men to Yourself [John 12:32]; so, Lord, I'm going to put all this in Your hands. You can do as You please with him."

By that time, we were approaching the customs' gate at the border between the United States and Canada.

"Citizenship?" the officer barked at me through my open window when I slowed to a stop.

"United States," I said.

"Canadian," the young man answered for his part.

"Pull over to the marshal's office," we were instructed.

Following that order, we were asked to take our luggage into the office for inspection. It was some inconvenience, but the weapons hanging at the sides of the uniformed officers didn't look as if they were just for decoration. It was best to follow instructions without complaint. Besides, I had nothing to hide.

It turned out they weren't remotely interested in me, at first.

"Where are you going?" they asked my passenger, giving him a real eagle eye.

"To Minnesota to work in a factory," he said.

"That's not what he told me!" I wanted to holler, but thought I should stay out of it. About then a whole carillon of bells was going off inside my cranium. Further down, the Spirit within was praying up a storm, interceding for me with groanings too deep for utterance (Romans 8:26). I was thankful Someone was on the hot line to heaven on my behalf; it looked as if I'd need all the help I could get.

Meanwhile, a marshal pulled a paper from a file, read it over, looked at the boy, read some more, looked some more, then broke the silence with an order: "Open your bag."

The boy opened it, and the officers crowded around, inspecting every seam on every piece of his clothing. Their inspection was so thorough, gnats on a fruit fly couldn't have escaped their scrutiny.

"Looks like trouble, Lord. How are You going to get me out of it?" My brooding on 2 Samuel 22:20 cranked into high gear: ". . . he delivered me, because he delighted in me."

My brooding did another gigantic leap forward when the biggest marshal took me aside, stared right through me, and asked, in as accusing a voice as I'd ever heard, "How long have you known this young man?"

"J-j-just a f-f-few m-m-minutes, s-s-s-sir. N-n-never laid eyes on h-h-him b-b-before I picked him up d-d-down the r-r-road a piece."

"Did you know that if he's a criminal, you're one, too, for trying to transport him across the border?"

I gulped. I had heard of such a thing, but being reminded of it in those circumstances impressed it on my memory in a brand-new way: indelible. I wouldn't forget it.

"You had better hope we can't prove anything on him, because if we do, you're headed for federal prison along with him."

I stood there, shaking, hoping my heart out. It's a good thing that praising the Lord is what I do best, because at that point, effective action was needed, not any futile, spinning-the-wheels stuff.

When another marshal came out with another incriminating looking document and searched through *my* bag for a solid hour, I could feel the old man of my senses trying to have his way, wanting to make me nervous, wanting to talk me into brooding about how felons don't get to make phone calls to anybody, how they lose their citizenship until they're proved innocent, which could take a while. Six months from now, my wife could be wondering why I never showed up from my trip across the border. Maybe she'd send out a posse to see if they could find a skeleton the timber wolves had left behind somewhere in the Canadian Rockies.

Whew! I couldn't afford to think of those things! In the nick of time, a positive attitude toward the Word of God came to my rescue. I reminded my old man that he was dead (Romans 6:11) and that he ought to act like it. I reminded myself that I was risen with Christ in God (Colossians 2:12), and that death had no power over me (1 Corinthians 15:54, 55). It took all I could give in terms of brooding on the promises of God to lift me up from shoelace level. But the Word worked, and I was back where King's kids belong: in an attitude of victory over the circumstances.

"Lord, I'm supposed to be home tonight. What are You going to do about it?" I *knew* He would do something, because His Word promised, "And call upon me in the day of trouble: I will deliver thee, and thou shalt glorify me" (Psalms 50:15).

I was certainly glad for His Word inside me. Otherwise, I'd have had no antidote for the circumstances He had allowed in order to let me learn a lesson.

"Hill, did you consult Me about the advisability of picking up this particular hitchhiker? Or were you leaning on your own understanding?"

"Touché, Lord, touché. I admit I didn't ask You. That was sin, Lord. I confess it. Please clean me of any tendency in that direction, according to Your promise: 'If we confess our sins, he is faithful and just and will forgive us our sins and purify us from all unrighteousness' [1 John 1:9 NIV]."

"You're repenting then, Hill?"

"Yes, Lord, I really blew it. Furthermore, Lord, I give You my permission to do whatever You want to do in this situation. If You want me to go to prison, it's fine with me. I'm just going to praise You, no matter what."

When I released it entirely to Him, getting rid of all striving and sweating about it myself—which couldn't do any good anyway—I felt the flood of His peace, like a river. What I loosed on earth was loosed in heaven (Matthew 16:19). It was as if I was holding the keys of the Kingdom of heaven in my hand, and I could almost hear the angels whooshing a gigantic sigh of relief, "Thank God, he got out from under that one!"

I still don't know how the Lord did it: whether He closed the senses of the marshals, so they couldn't see, smell, hear, or feel the evidence of the young man's guilt, whether He just evaporated the contraband, or what. The smirk on the fellow's face proved his guilt to me, but that wasn't something marshals could present to a jury, so they had to let him go after three or four hours of taking our luggage apart.

When it was finished, I knew the power of the Word in a new way: It has the strength to deliver us from fear and to keep us from getting in scary situations in the first place if we'll only be obedient to it. I knew, too, that the "all things" of Romans 8:28 applied to United States marshals and impending penitentiary sentences for King's kids in training. I must have needed to know those things, or the Lord wouldn't have allowed it to happen. Besides the improvement in my prayer life, I knew I'd never pick up a hitchhiker again unless it was the Lord's idea. Leaning on my own understanding belonged on the garbage heap.

I was living in high victory by the time the marshals took themselves into a corner for a conference—or a coin-tossing decision—then filed up to us and announced, "You are free to leave."

I said, "Thank you, sirs," and made tracks for the car.

The young man said thanks, too, but reading between the lines, the marshals and I knew he was really jeering, "You didn't find it, did you?"

How come they didn't find anything? Maybe God had sent a cover-up angel to hide dope or diamonds and so keep me out of bad trouble. Whatever He'd done, my attitude was one of thanksgiving.

"But didn't it bother you that a criminal got away with something?" someone is sure to ask.

"Not a bit," I can assure him. Why? Because another Scripture says, "There is nothing concealed that will not be disclosed, or hidden that will not be made known" (Luke 12:2 NIV).

The Scripture doesn't say *when* the loot will be discovered. There's a fullness-of-time factor in all these things. I'm just grateful God didn't choose to expose anything at a time that might have incriminated me. I appreciated His special arrangement for His King's kid and told Him so while I walked to the car.

The young man trailed after me, the smirk still on his face, as if he expected to continue his journey under the protection of my God. But I had learned my lesson.

"This is as far as we travel together," I told him.

He didn't argue or try to change my mind, just mumbled, "I understand," and headed down the road for a convenient place to hang out his thumb.

And so ended what could have been a permanently nerve-racking situation. If I hadn't known Jesus, I could have been worried in the midst of the proceedings. If I had known Jesus but had refused to praise God in the midst of things, or if I had been ignorant of the Scriptures that could lift me above the circumstances, I might have gnawed my fingernails down to the elbows—with good cause. As it was, praise put me back on the wavelength of heaven where God could bring His Word into fulfillment.

I still have a long way to go to arrive at perfection in this life of the Spirit, living the Bible. But I'm learning as I go along. And I'm persuaded that I'll reach my goal before the end of eternity. How come? Again, I have God's Word for it: "Being confident of this very thing, that he which hath begun a good work in you will perform it until the day of Jesus Christ" (Philippians 1:6).

Hallelujah that He never gives up on us. But I couldn't blame Him if He did. In all honesty, I haven't *intended* to present a special challenge to Him, but that's how it's turned out on more than one occasion.

Take the time when He wanted me to learn about meekness, for instance. . . .

7

The Case of the Lost Contract

When I was just beginning to learn how to live the Bible, I really rebelled at the be-attitudes, especially the one that said, "Blessed are the meek: for they shall inherit the earth" (Matthew 5:5).

I didn't have anything against inheriting the earth—that part sounded all right. But the thought of having to be a vegetable to do it, of having to lie down like a carrot and let other people walk all over me, went against my grain. And so the Lord in His mercy let me have some experiences in which I could learn that His way is the best, no matter how my senses might protest against it.

One such demonstration of the practical truth of His Word was especially rough on my ego. It came in connection with a large contract I was negotiating with a shipyard in Baltimore. I'd spent a lot of time working out the specifications for this particular piece of marine business, and the purchasing department had asked that I telephone them when I had everything ready for final negotiations.

When the appointed time came up on my calendar, I dialed the purchasing department and immediately felt as if I had been socked in my solar plexus.

"Mr. Hill, I'm sorry to say I have some bad news for you."

I knew better than to look at circumstances, but nonetheless, my feelings sunk to my sock tops.

"What bad news?" I squeaked, my throat suddenly as dry as an Elijah desert where it hadn't rained for three years and six months.

"We've decided to give that contract to a firm in New York City."

I don't recall what I *said* next—it might have been too hot for the telephone cable—but I well remember what I *did* next. I slammed the receiver of the phone down so hard it cracked the high-impact plastic.

Blessed are the meek? I was in a rage! The nerve of that outfit! I'd fix them! I'd show them they couldn't treat me that way and get by with it!

Before the Lord could say, "Wait a minute, Hill," I had brooded my initial disappointment into a murderous attitude. With all that angry adrenalin zooming through my system, I could have chopped that fellow into a million bite-sized pieces.

Then the Holy Spirit came to my rescue with that still small voice: "Is that the way I function in you, Hill? Have you forgotten that you're a container for Jesus, the Head Man of the universe? He never condemns anyone, does He?"

A verse came to my remembrance, loud and clear: "There is therefore now no condemnation to them which are in Christ Jesus, who walk not after the flesh, but after the Spirit" (Romans 8:1).

I knew I was still living in the flesh—the meat and bones with which I was born the first time—but there was a new life in me to prompt me in the right direction as far as my actions were concerned. That new life didn't try to force or coerce me, but just checked me when I was out of order, by a gentle tug at my gizzard. That tug will always get to you if your attitude toward the Lord is right, no matter how terribly you've behaved.

Immediately my spirit was on its knees: "Okay, Lord, I blew it again. He had it coming to him, but—"

There was the little tug again, reminding me that the fellow had a perfect right to award the contract where he thought best.

"Sorry, Lord. You'll have to be my righteousness in this, because I sure don't have any of my own."

I knew He *was* my righteousness, my wisdom, my sanctification, my redemption, my everything, because He said so in 1 Corinthians 1:30. What next? Confession, of course.

"Lord, I acted like a big baby. Thanks for forgiving me. What do You want me to do about it?"

I was hoping He'd say something easy, like, "That's all right. Just try not to let it happen again," and I'd be home free. But that isn't how He chose to handle it on that occasion. The Word that came to me was not what I wanted to hear:

> Therefore if thou bring thy gift to the altar, and there rememberest that they brother hath ought against thee;
> Leave there thy gift before the altar, and go thy way; first be reconciled to thy brother, and then come and offer thy gift.
>
> Matthew 5:23, 24

Along with it came another verse, equally unwelcome: ". . . let not the sun go down upon your wrath" (Ephesians 4:26).

He didn't have to remind me of the bodily consequences if I chose to nurse a resentment. I'd had too many dealings with arthritis in my pagan days ever to forget them. It was plain what I had to do, immediately, if I didn't want calamity in my joints. I'd have to humble myself, act meek. I'd go to the shipyard, hat in hand, and apologize for shattering the guy's eardrum with my phone slamming.

I asked God to make it easy for me; but He made it unforgettable instead, which was exactly what I needed.

When I arrived at the purchasing office, the man in charge was surrounded by eight key supervisory personnel. They had just finished an important management meeting, and unfortunately, all of them knew me.

"Come on in, Mr. Hill, come on in," Don boomed.

I edged into the door, sideways, hoping the rest wouldn't notice my presence, but would go on about their business so I could take care of mine.

No one ignored me; furthermore, they showed no signs of leaving.

The Holy Spirit was bugging me about getting on with it.

"But, Lord, in front of all these people? I mean, let's wait until they clear out. I'm willing to go the *second* mile, but making my apology in front of all these fellows will be the equivalent of an around-the-world marathon. It will make me a laughingstock. It's not fair!"

"Were you fair?" That still small voice wasn't going to quit; I could see that. It sounded as if it was going to get worse, so I took a deep breath and opened my mouth wide so God could fill it (Psalms 81:10).

"Don, I'm here to apologize for acting like an overgrown papoose. When you told me you'd decided to sign a contract with New York instead of with us, I reacted like a pagan. I want to ask your forgiveness for slamming the phone in your ear and having murderous thoughts toward you."

There, it was finished, and so was I. If the Lord hadn't upheld me by His right hand (Isaiah 41:10), I'd have landed on the carpet.

"No problem, Hill. Happens to us all. But you didn't give me time to deliver the *good* news. I have another contract here—one that's just right for your outfit—and it's four times the size of the one we placed in New York."

I heard the rest of his announcement from a distance, being seated in heavenly places, inheriting the Kingdom along with the rest of the meek.

"Take the contract along with you, Hill," he said, "and give me a call to let me know your bid. We'd like you to start supplying the equipment as soon as you can, without waiting for formalities."

I don't know whether I ever said thank-you to Don for that or not. I was too busy talking to the Lord.

"Jesus, You didn't have to do all that! Why, that's above all I could ask or think—"

"Isn't that exactly what I promised you in My Word," He seemed to ask me, *"when* you follow My directions and do it My way?"

"Yes, Lord. And thanks, Lord."

That's the day I found out that being meek isn't a down-the-drain deal after all. In fact, every one of the be-attitudes is the best attitude to have, an avenue to His riches in glory in the here and now—His Kingdom on earth as it is in heaven.

Funny thing about God's Word. It *generally* works just backward from how common sense figures it will. Come to think of it, God said it would be that way:

> For my thoughts are not your thoughts, neither are your
> ways my ways, saith the Lord. For as the heavens are higher
> than the earth, so are my ways higher than your ways, and
> my thoughts than your thoughts.
>
> Isaiah 55:8, 9

That's why it's so important to get the Word down inside us and let it work in our lives. After all, how can we know when we're operating according to His will if we don't know what His will is? The answer is, "We can't." But there's a remedy for that, too.

8

The Case of the Left-handed Map

"How can I know I'm in the will of God?" King's kids are always asking me.

"Read His Word and do it," I tell them. And then I give them a quick rule of thumb: "You're God's will in action whenever you're praising Him in the midst of what's going on. An attitude of rejoicing, praising, and thanksgiving always pleases God."

If they ask me for Scripture to back that up, I give them the Word God gave me way back in the beginning of my King's-kid life: "Rejoice evermore. Pray without ceasing. In every thing give thanks: for this is the will of God in Christ Jesus concerning you" (1 Thessalonians 5:16–18).

How does that work? In lots of different ways.

Take the night Brother Dick and I were headed for another meeting way out in the boondocks. We weren't familiar with the location of the new fellowship of believers who had invited us, and the

homemade map that had been sent to direct our paths was definitely
not of Rand McNally quality. To top it off, the mapmaker must have
been a southpaw, because every time we tried to get our bearings,
the roads were exactly backward from the way they appeared on the
paper.

After winding up at the fourth dead end in a row, we turned
around, praising the Lord, of course, and drove back to a four-way
intersection that was obviously not on the map at all. The roads had
names, plainly lettered on a tall marker, but not one of the names
appeared on the map. It looked as if we were entirely out of our
territory.

It was dark by that time; we'd lost track of where we came from;
and we had no clue as to what we should do next. But we knew we
wanted to continue in His will, so we continued to praise the Lord. It
even seemed in order to ask Him to send us guidance by whatever
method seemed appropriate to Him. That time, I certainly knew
better than to ask Him for a copilot in the form of a hitchhiker. I had
learned *one* lesson, at least.

"Lord, give us a word of encouragement," I prayed, and instantly
a verse from Hebrews popped into my mind: "Are not all angels
ministering spirits sent to serve those who will inherit salvation?"
(Hebrews 1:14 NIV).

"Thanks, Lord. Thanks for reminding us that we're heirs to
salvation, so we can expect You to save us from the lost condition in
which we find ourselves at the moment." The Scripture that came to
mind along with that thought was so good I could hardly keep from
shouting: "He that spared not his own Son, but delivered him up for
us all, how shall he not with him also freely give us all things?"
(Romans 8:32).

The "all things" that He was going to give us would have to
include the "all things" He was working together for good in Romans
8:28, so I knew we were about to have all we needed for our direction.
It was exciting just to sit there and praise the Lord for what He was
going to do next.

What I'm going to tell you now, I wouldn't have believed if I hadn't been there and seen it for myself. For about three minutes, Dick and I sat there at the mystery intersection and praised the Lord for His guidance, any way He wanted to send it. Then I became aware of headlights moving up in my rearview mirror. When the lights got to our location, the vehicle that belonged to them—a white VW bug—pulled ahead of us and stopped, signaling a left turn. Before it could move, a white Ford station wagon came out of nowhere, pulled up behind the VW, and signaled a left turn.

Dick and I were staring at each other, because we hadn't seen or heard another car for miles, and now there were two of them within breathing distance. But that wasn't all. A third white car, a four-door sedan of a model neither of us recognized, joined the parade, also signaling a left turn.

"Do you suppose they're three witnesses confirming that we're to turn left?" I asked Dick.

"Wait a minute," he said, as bug-eyed as I was. "Let's see if they're really going to turn, or if this is some kind of hallucination."

I knew it couldn't be a hallucination, because both of us were having it at the same time, and hallucinations are usually tailor-made to suit a single customer.

While we waited, the three cars moved as one, as if they were hitched together, disappearing around a slight curve down the left-hand road.

"Sic 'em for Jesus," Dick said, and we were on our way after them.

Funny thing, though. When we got around the bend in the road, there wasn't another car in sight. The road lay straight ahead, with no sign of a taillight anywhere.

A few miles down the road, there was a churchyard, however, with a number of cars that must have been gathering from another direction. It was the place where our meeting was scheduled, but there wasn't a white car in the lot.

What happened? Who knows? You tell me. We were lost, we prayed and praised the Lord, claiming His Word, and suddenly we were not lost.

Were angel cars sent to minister to us heirs to salvation? Could be. All I know is, God found a way to meet our need because we stayed in His will and trusted Him to help us in His way.

Will this method work for every King's kid? I can't say. You'll have to try it for yourself. His Word works for me wherever I try it, even in the uttermost parts of the earth, as long as I have the right attitude.

Soon after the Lord had started me down the brooding path, He sent me to Europe for such a whirlwind series of adventures over there that I've hardly caught my breath since. Some days, I learned more than I wanted to know!

9

The Case of the Missing Sword

The overseas brooding adventures of this particular King's kid learning how to live the Bible began one fall in early October when I headed out for my annual trip of witnessing in Europe—to brag on Jesus in Germany, Switzerland, and Austria. During the course of my journey, a lot of things happened that the world would call adversities, trials, or tribulations, but when I brooded on the Word of God about them and applied that Word according to His instructions, things turned out better than if the calamities hadn't happened.

When I failed to follow His instructions and brooded on appearances, letting my attitude be affected by the evidence of my ordinary senses, woe was me! But more of that later, if I can get up the nerve to let you in on it. Having done some homework in God's Word, I knew in advance some of the principles I should apply for best results in Kingdom living: that I should consider every problem pure joy (James 1:2), that I should thank Him for all things (Ephesians 5:20), and that I should rejoice all the time (1 Thessalonians 5:16), praying without ceasing (1 Thessalonians 5:17), while I let patience have her perfect work in me (James 1:4).

I knew these things, and many more, because I had salted the Scriptures down in my gizzard for use whenever the Lord told me to put them into action. The Holy Spirit is always teaching me principles in the Word, and then Jesus lets circumstances come about to give me a chance to put the Word in action and get a real handle on each principle for myself through an actual adventure—like a laboratory experiment confirming the fact.

When I keep busy doing the Word, a few little tribulations—or even a whole flock of Goliath ones—don't send me off on a blubbery round of pity parties in which I get indigestion from gulping martyr pills. With the right attitude inside me, tribulation simply improves my prayer life and brings more glory to Jesus. Besides that, the Word says that my tribulations are going to result in my perfection:

> My brethren, count it all joy when ye fall into divers
> temptations; Knowing this, that the trying of your faith
> worketh patience. But let patience have her perfect work,
> that ye may be perfect and entire, wanting nothing.
>
> James 1:2-4

Now, I don't know about you, but I can hardly wait for that to happen to me!

The new crop of so-called adversities—really, raw material to make me perfect—got underway on a Thursday afternoon before I ever reached Baltimore-Washington International Airport for the first installment of the airborne part of my journey. Riding along in my car, I was suddenly aware of something missing on the upper half of my torso. A systematic search was plainly in order.

Looking down to see what was lacking, so I could begin to praise God that He could supply whatever I needed, I saw that my sleeves were full, both arms still attached, intact, in proper working order, and adequately appendaged.

I had all my buttons.

Checking my lapel, I saw that I hadn't forgotten to wear my I AM A KING'S KID pin. It was in its usual position, deliberately upside down so folks would mention it innocently, opening the door for me to tell them I was upside down, too, until Jesus turned me right side up. With that for openers, such conversation *could* lead to conversions—and often had.

Next, I started patting my pockets, taking inventory of their contents:

One skinny billfold
A passport, properly visaed
Spectacles to wear for reading fine print, until Jesus gives me back twenty-twenty vision for close range, as He has already given me for distance viewing
A clean handkerchief

Whoops! There was something missing, all right. I couldn't feel the familiar bulge of the New Testament with the Psalms that I always carry in the pocket over my heart. I must have left it at home.

I knew right away that it wasn't an accident, because there are no accidents in the lives of King's kids. Somewhere, somehow, the Lord had real glory for Himself and real joy for me stored up concerning that situation.

"One, two, three. . . ," I started counting the joy already as the Manufacturer's Handbook instructed me to do (James 1:2), knowing that if I would incubate it properly, brood on it continually, and keep the right attitude, joy would hatch out sooner or later.

That I left my New Testament at home didn't mean that I was without any weapon at all. I had a full-length sword of the Spirit

(Hebrews 4:12) safely tucked away in my luggage, but I felt half naked without my quick-draw shootin' iron in its holster.

Feeling naked didn't seem to be God's best for me, any more than it had been for Granddaddy Adam before God made the first fur-lined snuggies for him in Eden Gardens, so I sent up a quick prayer, based on the Word that God brought to my remembrance. My appeal to heavenly headquarters went something like this:

"Lord, Your Word says You'll supply all my needs out of Your riches in glory by Christ Jesus [Philippians 4:19] and You'll even give me the desires of my heart [Psalms 37:4]. Lord, my heart's desire is to have a little New Testament in my breast pocket. I know I can buy a German one when I get to Germany, but I can't read German all that well, so I'd like to have one in English, please."

That completed the specifications of my requisition, and because I believed the Word of God was true, I knew He'd fill my holster in the fullness of time, in His way.

Having a few minutes to spare between planes at New York's Kennedy International Airport, I checked some gift shops and bookstores there, but when I asked the clerks, "Do you have a pocket New Testament for me?" most of them said, "Huh?" as if they'd never heard of such a thing.

While I buckled my seatbelt on the 747 for the overseas flight, I put the whole matter completely in His hands: "Lord, my shopping trip back there was a wild-goose chase, but I thank You that in the right time and place, You'll bring me a New Testament. Amen."

I knew He would do it because I wanted it for His glory and not mine. But if He'd told me ahead of time all I'd have to go through in order to collect on my prayer, I'd have chickened out with, "Never mind, Lord. Please cancel the order." But He didn't let on that anything out of the ordinary would be involved, so I didn't suspect a thing. Was I in for some surprises!

Meanwhile, after I left the New Testament order with headquarters and brooded on it joyfully in my spare time, the Lord let me have a *tough* piece of tribulation to chew on. Counting *it* all joy wasn't quite so easy.

10

Ordeal in Agony

The fellow in the terminal who assigned my seat for the overseas flight must have mistaken me for a pretzel, because he put me in a piece of upholstery plainly designed for a contortionist instead of for a hunk of humanity with bones and muscles in all the conventional places. Furthermore, I had a cold, gray bulkhead for a seatmate, instead of a warm somebody who could listen to me brag on Jesus. Because of the inflexible anatomy of the bulkhead, it was necessary for me to twist myself into a pretzel shape and sit more or less sidesaddle to accommodate my contours to those of my silent traveling companion for the long overwater flight.

When I hobbled off the plane in Frankfurt, Germany, the next morning, my torso was a little touchy, to say the least—all warped and sore and sensitive on the left side. To put it more bluntly, I was in considerable pain. What to do about it? Why, standard order of procedure was indicated, of course: praise the Lord and do the next thing. So I began praising the Lord for ribs to give me pain. Then I praised Him for the muscles that were giving me spasms to go along with the pain. And I praised Him for nerve circuits to keep all the agony in constant contact with my brain.

I praised Him for a brain. After all, it would usually be bad *not* to have ribs or muscles or nerves or a brain. Hurting pieces of anatomy were probably better than none at all, I reasoned—though I wasn't too sure of that at the moment—so I praised Him for what I had and went on to do the next thing. That was *not* to make arrangements to rest my ribs, to massage my muscles, or to catch up on the five hours' worth of jet lag I had logged by flying in a direction opposite to the sun, but to visit the German publisher of my books. It was a long and busy day, that Friday.

On Saturday, all the pains and spasms got worse. By the time Sunday arrived, I was in pretty bad shape before breakfast and in even more terrible shape after I had spoken for a couple of hours in two different King's-kid meetings in the big opera house at Karlsruhe. My interpreter spoke for more than equal time, naturally, some German words being six syllables longer than their English equivalents.

When all the doubletalk was over for the day, my torso was threatening to leave me. I couldn't blame it. The feeling was mutual. Both of us really needed to get horizontal for a good night's rest before heading for tomorrow's assignment: an FGBMFI meeting down the road in Stuttgart.

But I discovered other plans were afoot when someone marched up to me immediately after the Sunday-afternoon meeting and said a car was waiting to take me to Stuttgart right away.

"Are you ready for the trip?" the cheery driver wanted to know.

If I hadn't written a book once upon a time in which I called people "Billy-goat Christians" for saying, "Yes, but—" I might have said it myself. As it was, I smiled, nodded, kept my mouth shut, picked up my suitcase, and followed the man.

On the way to the car, I prayed, "Okay, Lord. It's entirely up to You. I thought I needed to get in bed to rest before I fall apart, but I praise You that You'll take care of my aching torso some other way."

I didn't think I needed to tell God the situation was getting worse by the minute, that my muscles were all knotted up under my ribs like a charley horse. I knew He had it all under control. Since I knew His Word could sort out the thoughts and intents of my heart (Hebrews 4:12), it was reasonable to assume that His X-ray eyes could also diagnose my assorted aches and pains without getting a certified laboratory report.

I did think a tiny reminder might be in order, however, so I delivered it as plainly as I knew how: "Lord, please be sure to leave me enough breath to praise You, because You said that everything that had breath is to praise the Lord continually [Hebrews 13:15; and Psalms 150:6], and I want to be obedient to every Word that comes from Your mouth. If the pain gets any worse, so I can't get my breath at all, You'll get short-changed in the praise department, and I'll fall off the wavelength of heaven. I wouldn't want that to happen, but it's Your problem, Lord. Do whatever suits You about it."

Well, that temporarily took care of the breathing difficulty, but when I saw the vehicle that was to transport me to Stuttgart, I did a double take. And I almost wished for the relative comfort of an airplane seat designed for a pretzel and shared with a bulkhead.

11

Agony Compounded

The wheels that had come to transport me to Stuttgart were axled under the babiest VW Rabbit I'd ever seen! I knew the engineers were miniaturizing everything these days, but I never dreamed they'd get around to motorizing Tonka toys for super-highway traffic. Since in all my adult life I've never been less than six feet tall, it was going to take some powerful accordion pleating and a giant-sized shoehorn to stuff me into the front seat. I didn't know how my charley-horsed rib cage was going to feel about that. So far, it didn't feel good about anything, so I was confident it wasn't going to take the trip lying down. In fact, I was certain of it. There was no way a Barbie doll could have gotten horizontal in that car without poking her spike heels through the windshield and resting her head on the exhaust pipe in the rear, or vice versa.

But the directions in the Manufacturer's Handbook didn't say anything about turning down the hallelujahs when vehicular accommodations were less than limousine, so I continued to praise Him. It was actually easy to do when I considered the alternatives to the tiny transportation.

"Lord, I really praise You for this set of wheels. After all, Lord, it's better than roller skates—has a roof, in case of rain. And the tires aren't flat. Besides, I remember that You rode a donkey. Why, You could have sent a mean, slow, bony, old fodder furnace to pick me up, instead of this nice, friendly, upholstered piece of fifty-miles-per-hour Rabbit power. You're so *thoughtful*, Lord, You think of absolutely everything! Why, if we run out of Rabbit fuel or have any kind of mechanical mishap, it'll be a cinch to carry the Rabbit the rest of the way in my hip pocket."

And so I continued to thank the Lord for everything I could think of and to put joy numbers on all my apparent troubles:

Joy number one: the fact that I was going to Stuttgart now instead of tomorrow morning after I had rested

Joy number two: the fact that my ribs and muscles were arguing about which hurt the most

Joy number three: the fact that I had barely enough breath to praise Him for the Rabbit that was going to parade six feet two of accordion-pleated pachyderm down the highway

I was singing His praises along those lines while I was cramming myself into the passenger side of the front seat. As soon as I thought I'd made it, I grabbed for the door to slam it shut before any of me squished back outside. That was a bad move!

In all my contortions to get all of me crunched into the space that wasn't quite big enough to hold a family-sized box of Cheerios, I'd failed to notice that my thumb was still halfway outside the car. When I slammed the door, the nerves of my thumb let me know—faster than the speed of sound—that the shattering noise I was about to hear was directly related to the total pulverization of bones and flesh in their immediate vicinity. *Ouch!*

Did I continue to praise the Lord? Of course. What else? Matter of fact, it was easy—automatic. In such circumstances a King's kid doesn't have to *decide* what to do. King's kids are programmed to praise Him, no matter what, and instinctive reactions took over.

Admittedly, my praising was kind of jagged there for a few minutes, punctuated with some equally instinctive and permissible sounds of agony. Intermittent praising is acceptable when a close-fitting door has slammed, metal to metal, with your own flesh and blood as filling in the sandwich.

While some of my reflexes were praising the Lord, thanking Him that I *had* a thumb to mash in the door in the first place (though whether I still had that particular thumb was temporarily open to question), and thanking Him for whatever He could do with the damaged leftovers, short of consigning them to a compost heap, other reflexes shoved the door open in Olympic-medal time.

I didn't dare look at what was left of the most vital digit on my right hand. I just grabbed hold of it with my left hand and covered it with the healing stripes of Jesus before total destruction could claim His property for keeps. While I hollered to my thumb, "The maimed were made whole! The maimed were made whole!" from Matthew 15:31, and prayed some further perfection into it with words I couldn't understand, my thumb was throbbing pain back at me like the loudest Indian tom-tom ever given a decibel rating.

But I couldn't afford to pay any attention to thumb talk. That would fog my signals from heaven, set up static that would interfere with my reception of heaven's best. I had to keep thinking of things of *good* report, especially Jesus, who promised He'd keep me in perfect peace, *if* I'd keep my mind on Him (Isaiah 26:3) and not lean on my own understanding (Proverbs 3:5). Perfect peace was what I needed, all right, so I kept thanking Jesus and praising Him for whatever shred of my appendage was left. I knew that as long as I thanked Him, nothing could happen to me that was not His will in Christ Jesus concerning me (1 Thessalonians 5:18). Furthermore, I knew it was not His will for me to perish (2 Peter 3:9), whether I felt like it or not.

Besides all that, His Word rose up to remind me it wasn't His will that ". . . one of these little ones should perish"(Matthew 18:14), and my thumb seemed to fit the description. So I kept on praising Him, but it wasn't exactly easy.

12

Uptight Versus Loosed in Heaven

If I'd been relying on the evidence of my senses, I couldn't have believed that the particular circumstances in which I found myself that day could possibly have been God's will for me. They didn't *feel* joyful, but His Word said I was to count them all joy if I wanted to be perfected (James 1:2–4).

Did I want to be perfected? Something inside me said that perfection included a perfect thumb. That was worth holding on for.

Did praising the Lord work? Of course it did. It always does, not when we just think about it, but when we do it, because God dwells in the praises of His people (Psalms 22:3); and where He is, no imperfection can stand.

Proof? I still have my thumb intact, a working model, with a brand-new, pink thumbnail and a testimony to match: that the Lord can restore crushed thumb bones. How would I have known that for sure if I hadn't experienced it for myself? The next time I read the question in Ezekiel 37:3, ". . . can these bones live? . . ." I had my own personal answer: "Amen!"

Putting joy numbers on my pulverized thumb made me temporarily forget all about the charley horse galloping around in my chest like a Thoroughbred in training for the Kentucky Derby. For about an hour, I wasn't even *aware* of the horse race, because of the spasm my thumb was enduring to get all jiggled back into perfect alignment for healing. But after the hour was up, when my thumb nerves had worked themselves into a state of total exhaustion, I turned the lion's share of the praising back to ribs and chest muscles again.

Several light years later, when we arrived at Stuttgart, some angels of mercy performed a Hill-ectomy on the Rabbit, practically carried me into the mission station, and tucked me in bed, packing me down with hot-water bottles and ice packs. Sometime during the night when their temperatures had equalized so I was neither blistered nor frozen, my nerves had revived enough to have another go at reminding me of my ailments. The pain impulses revved up to such a state that if I hadn't *known* God was working in all things for good, I might have complained out loud once in a while. As it was, I kept being thankful for the first three words of Romans 8:28—"And we *know*"—that wiped out all doubt from my attitude, while I kept doing 1 Thessalonians 5:17: thanking and praising Him, not questioning why He was letting me go through such misery.

But by about four o'clock in the morning, I had completed my quota. I was out of breath for praising, counting joy, or doing anything else. It was time for some straight talk, so I let Him have it: "Lord, meaning no disrespect—moan, groan—but this is so bad—moan, groan—that if You don't do something—moan, groan—I'm going to have to call for—moan, groan—medical attention. Frankly, Lord—moan, groan—at this point, a nice tight tourniquet—moan, groan—around my neck—moan, groan—would be a relief—moan, groan."

I told Him flatly that if He, the Great Physician, didn't make His rounds before daylight, I was going to see a German doctor. Putting it all freshly in His hands with the pronouncement, "Lord, it's Your bag," I turned over and fell sound asleep.

Without even thinking about it, I'd unleashed· a powerful spiritual principle I'd known for years: What you loose on earth—by detaching yourself from it emotionally—is loosed in heaven (Matthew 18:18). I had been binding myself up in my misery, because I was so closely attached to it. But when I loosed it to Him, He gave His beloved sleep. Funny I hadn't asked Him to do that already, since it had worked so well in Jack's case, back in Baltimore. But that's the way it is with me. Some things, the Lord has to teach me more than once.

13

Texas in Europe

"ZZZzzzZzzzZzzz—"

Along about dawn, the room was echoing with the reverberations of someone snoring up a storm when a loud knock at the door woke me up. In the next moment, a man walked in, tall as the ceiling.

"Good morning, Brother Hill," he boomed, in the most authentic Texas accent I'd ever heard east of the Atlantic. "I'm Nick Gurick, missionary from Haiti. My home is in Texas, and I'm due to preach in Yugoslavia tonight; but in the meantime, I understand you have a problem." Quite an introduction for six o'clock in the morning, before the birds were up looking for worms.

"You could call it a problem," I admitted. "My back is all knotted up like macrame, and I can neither breathe nor move without calling out the rescue squad."

"No *real* problem, then," he grinned, and for a minute I thought I was hearing a hallucination. I mean, I couldn't breathe or move, and he thought I had no problem? He *looked* smarter than that.

But then he explained. "Before I became a missionary, I was a professional masseur, specializing in muscle spasms of the rib cage. That seems to be your diagnosis."

"On the button." I nodded my head so vigorously it almost fell off.

"Please pardon me for barging in so early," he apologized, "but I've got to catch a plane for Belgrade, so whatever I'm going to do for you, I've got to do right away."

"The sooner the better," I whispered, my strength shot. "Immediately is none too soon as far as I'm concerned."

Telling me to lie still—as if he thought I entertained other notions—he went out to get some rubbing alcohol so he could start work right away. But it took him a little longer than he figured to get the ingredients. The druggists all told him they didn't carry such a thing. All their alcohol was meant for internal consumption.

"Well," he finally asked the last druggist in town, "what *do* you use to rub down athletes when they have muscle spasms?"

At that, the druggist's eyes lit up like a pinball machine. "Ah! Ve haf athlete liniment!" he exclaimed.

It was all a matter of asking the right question. The fine print on the bottle assured Nick the content was rubbing alcohol, whether the druggist knew it or not, so he brought it in, took off his coat, rolled up his sleeves, uncorked the jug, and started in on me.

"I'll have you on your feet in an hour," he promised.

It sounded preposterous, almost as if he was expecting a resurrection from the dead; and what he did *felt* preposterous, too. If I'd had eyes in the back of my head, I could probably tell you what went on, unless I'd fainted at the sight. I *think* he jumped up and down on my back—with cleats—wrenched it first one way and then another, breaking all my ribs loose from their muscle moorings and ripping the muscles from their nerve endings. For a while, my back thought the awful pain I'd suffered during the night was a Sunday-school picnic compared to this mob guerilla warfare—with me, all by myself, as the whole enemy. If Nick hadn't sounded so friendly, I'd have hollered for the police.

I still don't know which was worse: what I had or what he did with it.

Think I'm exaggerating? Have you ever had all *your* cells unglued at once? If I'd been going by my feelings, I'd have opted for a quick decapitation to get out of my misery, but I was going by faith that when he said he'd have me on my feet in an hour, he knew what he was talking about.

He did.

While Nick prayed in the Spirit, I praised the Lord in English, and before the hour was up, so was I.

Nick collapsed in a chair to recover from my operation, but I could stand up and breathe—both at the same time. Highly satisfactory outcome—and he didn't charge me a cent.

"How'd you happen to come by?" I asked him when he got up to leave.

"Oh, I'd heard that Sister Paula, the pastor in charge of this church, had had a massive heart attack a few weeks ago, and the doc said she couldn't live, but the brethren had prayed her back on her feet. So I just dropped by to add my prayers to the collection and to praise the Lord for her continuing recovery. That's when she told me you were in worse shape than she was, so—"

With that, he shook my hand and took off, his Texas-sized boots eating up the length of the long hall almost before I could say thanks. My mind was still wobbling, just thinking about the *special* special treatment the King gives to His kids. I'd known Him to do some pretty wonderful things, but what had just happened strained even my credulity a little:

a Texas preacher
  on his way to Yugoslavia
    by way of Haiti
      stopping by Stuttgart
        to pray for a German pastor
          just in time to use his specialty in muscle spasms
            on a Baltimore engineer
              who needed to get on his feet
                for a Full Gospel meeting.

That combination of coincidences in faraway places could make a believer out of anybody.

But the best was yet to come.

14

Ask and It Shall Be Given . . .

While I stood there, praising the Lord and buttoning my shirt, another booming voice shattered my eardrums.

"Praise the Lord, Brother Hill!"

"I'm already doing it," I told the man barging out of the room next to mine. Turned out he was Brother Steyn, a completed Jew (that means he knows his Messiah has already come and that His name is Jesus) from New London, South Africa. Like the tall Texan, he was on his way to catch a plane, but had stopped by for a minute to say hello to Sister Paula on his way through. He'd read my books, he said, and had been wanting to shake my hand and invite me down to South Africa.

"When can you come?"

As I dug my engagement book out of my pocket to check dates, I saw several reasons why the Lord had me come to Stuttgart the night before, instead of waiting to arrive just in time for the evening

meeting today. Why, I'd have missed the rib-cage masseur who got
me on my feet *and* the South African invitation, to say nothing about
the frosting on the cake that was about to wind the whole thing up, full
circle, with a tailor-made answer to prayer. Have you guessed what it
was? I couldn't have figured it out myself.

"Let's have a little word of prayer together with Sister Paula
before I blast off," Brother Steyn said after we'd settled on a time for
my South African visit. "And while we're at it, let's share a little
teaching from the Word."

All that was quite agreeable with me, of course. We went to
Sister Paula's quarters, laid hands on her, and then they both laid
hands on me, brooding on God's promise that when believers lay
hands on the sick, they will recover (Mark 16:18). We had good Bible
authority for that, and because we'd all seen it work many times in
the past, it was easy for our attitudes to agree that it would work again.

After we finished our prayers for each other, getting excited
about our soon-to-be-manifested total recovery, my eyeballs nearly
rolled out of my head when Brother Steyn reached into his shirt
pocket over his heart and pulled out a familiar-looking little black
book and began to read out of it—in English.

After he finished reading, I just had to ask him a question:
"Brother Steyn, is that by any chance a New Testament—in
English?"

"Well, yes, but it's more than that," he said. "It's the New
Testament *and* the Psalms."

I told him that I'd left mine behind in the United States and
asked, "Do you happen to have any idea where I can find one of those
over here?"

He didn't bat an eye.

"No," he said, "I don't know where you can *find* one, but this one
doesn't happen to be lost, and it's for you."

He flashed me the biggest, whitest smile I'd ever seen while he
autographed the Bible for me, stuck it in the pocket over my ticker,
gave it a good-bye pat, and took off running for South Africa.

I could have taken off at a fast trot, myself, I felt so good, counting the joy of the trials I had gone through to get to the exact place where God had arranged to answer my prayer for a replacement New Testament. The Psalms were an above-all-I-had-asked bonus, according to Ephesians 3:20.

Was *anything* ever too hard for God? It didn't look like it. Once again, He'd brought total victory out of the most unlikely set of circumstances:

a seat designed for a pretzel
  an excruciating muscle spasm
    a miniature Rabbit to transport an ailing elephant
     a smashed thumb
      and all the rest of it

Now that they were over, I wouldn't have missed one of those adventures for anything.

"You mean you're actually willing to count it all joy, Hill?"

"Joy number one, joy number two, joy number three. . . , all the way to infinity, Lord," I answered, feeling rather smug and proud of myself for having lived through it all.

Well, He saw my heart, and how I was taking credit for my part in it, instead of giving all the glory to Him for providing the grace to endure. It must have been plain I had something else to learn about attitudes.

"Very well, Hill. Since you enjoy tribulations so much, I'll let you have a few more to work on in your spare time."

I smiled inside and out, knowing I could do all things through Him who strengtheneth me (Philippians 4:13). But I had temporarily forgotten to be humble. I was ignoring the truth of Ephesians 2:8, 9, where God says, "For by grace are ye saved through faith; and that not of yourselves: it is the gift of God, Not of works, lest any man should boast."

I was boasting, forgetting the be-attitude that said, "Blessed are the poor in spirit: for theirs is the kingdom of heaven" (Matthew 5:3).

Do I need to tell you? The next adventure wasn't exactly mountaintop all the way. But I did learn something new. There was something I'd need to know about brooding—if I survived.

15

Programmed for Trouble

When King's kids are on the job, they're either in trouble, just getting out of trouble, or getting ready to get into bigger trouble. Isn't that how it was with Paul? If you wanted to find him in a strange city, you didn't go looking in the swankiest hotel; you went to the dingiest pokey. And you didn't look for him to be living it up, twirling the keys of authority while sitting in a swivel chair in an air-conditioned administrator's office with a six-pack of something cold at his elbow and a color TV with pushbuttons at his command. You'd look for him—and find him—in the lowest dungeon, locked in the stocks, black and blue from beating, technicolor blood running down his back, and helicopter-sized mosquitoes eating him alive.

But was Paul complaining? Never! He was always rejoicing— couldn't keep from it, since he knew Jesus had come ". . . to set at liberty them that are bruised" (Luke 4:18). Brooding on the truth of that, he was as good as set free before the jailer had locked him in, pocketed his key, and climbed the stairs to finish his breakfast.

And what happened? Sometimes there was an earthquake, and the jailhouse came apart at the seams (Acts 16:26). The authorities could count on *not* keeping Brother Paul locked up for long. There was mighty power in his faith and in his praising God—resurrection power, he called it (Ephesians 1:19, 20). Why, because he had the right attitude toward the Word of God, Paul could brood up an effortless, no-fault jailbreak quicker than most folks could crack a boiled, soft-shelled peanut. Furthermore, he'd get the jailer and his whole family—servants and all—saved in the process (Acts 16:28–34).

Now, I don't want to mislead anyone into thinking that I ever got locked up in the same way Paul did, or that I behaved in the same admirable King's-kid manner, or that exactly the same kind of jailbreak happened to me, but I did find myself involved in an adventure in which I could really appreciate the fact that Jesus came to set the captives free.

This golden opportunity for a great learning experience came on a pitch-dark night after I had joined forces with Brother George Jesze as a speaker/interpreter package to brag on Jesus in a two-week series of meetings in Austria, Switzerland, and some nearby parts of Germany.

Brother Jesze is director of Europe's Voice of Renewal. He's a young King's kid, born in Poland during the war. His family got bombed out and went to England, where he grew up and got his education. For several years, Brother George pastored churches in Germany and Switzerland before entering his present ministry of evangelism and teaching.

George speaks half a dozen languages, better than the natives, and he knows some Russian, so he's a handy fellow to have along where other folks' English isn't too good.

I was especially glad to meet up with Brother George on this trip, because someone had just loaned him a brand-new Mercedes to use during our two weeks together. It felt so good to my abused anatomy to be able to ride stretched out instead of scrunched up that I didn't have to *try* to praise the Lord all the way to our first stop, which happened to be a picturesque little hotel at the edge of the Black Forest.

I was scheduled to speak at a local church that night, and we arrived in plenty of time for a long afternoon nap. It was easy to praise the Lord for that, too.

The hotel was what the travel brochures would call charming, built like a thirteenth-century castle of gray stone, with barred windows that wouldn't open, and massive, double-thick oak doors that creaked shut on great, rusted iron hinges. I was surprised *not* to find a moat full of alligators and a drawbridge complete with a portcullis to keep out invading enemy horsemen. But even without those refinements, it was an altogether interesting place, like another world.

Even more interesting, at first, was a strange custom they have in hotels in that part of the world which I hadn't encountered elsewhere in my travels. Twice a week, about noon, everybody takes a prolonged coffee break. The whole staff locks up, leaves the premises, and goes home, issuing the duly registered guests two keys: one to get in and out of their rooms, and the other to get in and out of the building. The custom is called rest days for the staff—they don't come back until morning—and could be called murder for guests at the hotel under certain circumstances.

As a matter of fact, I—world-renowned King's kid in action, bragging about being a winner, living in high victory—was about to be under the circumstances.

But I didn't know that until later, so I was still wearing my glory grin when George and I checked in and were issued our keys.

I took the key for our room, and George took the outside-door key. While I started down the hallway, George went back out to the car for some of his things, coming back in through a door the last vanishing staff member had left ajar for him so he wouldn't have to bother with a key on that trip. That particular act of consideration was going to boomerang, but we didn't know it yet.

Naturally, when George got back inside the hotel, he closed the door behind him, came to our room, took off his shoes, and stretched out on his bed for a siesta, according to the local custom. I konked out, too, knowing arrangements had already been made for a local preacher to come to the hotel at 7:45 to pick us up for the meeting.

Nothing for us to worry about, so we got busy snoring up a storm. If we'd only known. . . .

16

The Case of the Locked-Up Castle

All went perfectly well until George and I woke up, got slicked up for the evening, and ambled to the lobby, ready to greet the man who was to take us to the meeting. No problems.

But the lobby was empty as a billfold before payday. Still no problem. The preacher was probably waiting outside.

Five feet from the door, George stopped in his tracks and began to take inventory of his pockets. The look on his face told me he hadn't found what he was looking for.

"Brother Hill," he said, "we have a problem."

"A problem? Well, praise the Lord, Brother George!" I exclaimed, certain I could handle anything that came up. "I've had several problems so far on this trip. I've counted them all joy, and they've turned out so well, I can hardly wait to get to work praising the Lord for this one. Between the two of us, we can brood up a perfect solution in line with the Lord's promises. Since we've got the right attitude, it won't take long. Let's get going while you tell me all about it."

All unsuspecting, I strode over and grabbed hold of the giant-sized handle of the door and pulled, then pushed, then looked at George in amazement. He nodded his head at me.

"You've got the picture," he said. "This establishment isn't like your American hotels, where everything opens out and it's against the law for you to be locked in. Here, on rest days, you have to have the key if you want to go anywhere—in or out. Otherwise, you just stay put."

"You mean we're in the 'otherwise' position?" I asked him, rejoicing that I'd never had the opportunity to praise the Lord for exactly that circumstance before. "You mean you don't have the key?"

While he kept nodding his head at me, I cranked my praising into high gear and did the next thing, heading for the telephone hanging on the wall of the vestibule.

"This one's going to be too easy," I told him, being a little disappointed that we'd miss a *real* tribulation. "I'll just call some-body, and they'll come down and bring us a key and get us out."

I was wondering vaguely whom I'd call. I didn't know the name of a soul—oh, but George would know somebody, or the operator could help us out.

I wondered why George was just standing there, shaking his head in a negative direction now, but I found out as soon as I picked up the receiver and found it dead as a doornail. When I jiggled the phone to see if I could wake it up, George acquainted me with further facts: "On rest days, *everything* rests, Brother Hill. They even disconnect the switchboard before they leave the place. No calls in, no calls out. Rest—total rest. Praise the Lord."

Ordinarily, I'd have joined him, just as you would have expected based on my past history of praising Him for everything. But for the first time in my entire King's-kid life, I couldn't seem to crank it up. Talk about feeling peculiar!

I must have been looking cross-eyed, too, for a King's kid, because I was looking at the circumstances—never recommended—instead of at Jesus—always recommended. My attitude nose-dived into a tailspin.

"You mean we're stuck here with no way to contact the outside world?" I croaked at him. "And no groceries?" It had been a long time since lunch.

"That's about the size of it," George smiled, looking ready to whistle, not to whimper—hardly a rational reaction to our predicament.

Suddenly the ten-by-ten windowless vestibule seemed to be shrinking, the walls closing in on us. I figured if anybody had any tendencies toward claustrophobia, it was a perfect set-up for him to climb the walls in terror.

I thought about that a minute too long, and though I'd never experienced that particular affliction before, I began, creepingly, to know what claustrophobia felt like. Something inside tried to remind me that Paul and Silas in prison and Jonah in the whale came out all right, but trying to think about them didn't seem to help much. For some reason, I couldn't keep my mind on the things of good report.

Believe it or not, Harold Hill, King's kid, was coming down with a clear case of heebie-jeebies.

"Are you sure there's nobody around inside the building?" I begged George, my voice panicky.

"Sure I'm sure. They've all checked out—lock, stock, and barrel. Well, not quite that bad," he chuckled. "They've left the locks in place. Too bad, but praise the Lord anyway. Jesus can set the captives free. He's our Deliverer."

A fellow in our predicament making jokes about it? Unreal! I stared at George. He must be having roof trouble. With all the pressure, he must have flipped his lid already.

I didn't relish the thought of being locked up with a madman!

I didn't know the Richter ratings of the area, but I doubted it was in line for an earthquake, and I couldn't see a stone hotel suddenly getting an upchucky interior and depositing us out on dry land, as the whale did in Jonah's case. And for the life of me, I couldn't figure out any other way the Lord could arrange to rescue us.

Paul and Silas weren't released from their prison until along about midnight, as I recalled. That meant we had a good four hours yet to go, and a lunatic *could* become violent in that length of time. Besides, all the folks at the meeting, waiting to hear me speak, would have gone home long before then.

Brooding on the seed of panic I had let get planted inside me by looking at the circumstances instead of at God's Word, and by exalting the common-sense attitudes of my own intellect instead of exalting Jesus, I frantically started yanking at all the doors I could find.

Glory! One of them opened!

17

A Glimpse of the Bottomless Pit

Yes, a door opened, all right—into a dead-end freezer with tallowy sides of mutton hanging all over the place. Bare corpses of sheep were no help. I was almost frozen to death already. I could visualize myself drawn and quartered and hanging there alongside all that raw meat. The fact that sheep know the shepherd's voice was no comfort to me.

"Well, Lord," I heard George say, "if we can't brag on You at the meeting, we'll brag on You right here, where we are. We're just going to praise You because we've got the breath to do it."

That was the wrong thing for him to say. Not only did it prove he'd lost all his marbles, but it made me wonder how many cubic feet of air were in the building and how much we would require to breathe through the night. When you're in a place that's locked up tighter than a tick, with no openable windows, you can run out of oxygen if you're not careful. I started keeping my respiration as shallow as possible, so as not to waste a single breath.

By that time, George was really far out. He kept praising the Lord as if he expected Almighty God to do something! It was plain as our tomblike environs that he'd abandoned common sense entirely and was totally unaware of the gravity of our situation.

While I stood and shivered with dread, that crazy George informed me that he was going upstairs to poke around a little and see if he could find a trapdoor leading to the roof. I didn't waste any air telling him there was no way he could get *me* to climb out on a roof in the dark and break my neck, falling onto sharp cobblestones — meeting or no meeting. I'd seen folks in traction, and they'd never looked too comfortable. Why, one man I knew had broken his neck and *died* from it!

George went upstairs alone. I wondered how long a fellow could live with a broken neck and speculated about whether my hospitalization policy was good enough to cover the expense of being paralyzed the rest of my life. With practical nurses getting minimum wage and everything being unionized. . . .

It was grim, and the longer I thought, the gloomier the prospects seemed to be. I remembered that my will was up-to-date, but I couldn't even be glad about that.

Looking back, I see that I was being a perfect example of imperfection. Readers who have the Manufacturer's Handbook hid in their hearts will know that I should have been using the mighty weapons God gives us for "Casting down imaginations, and every high thing that exalteth itself against the knowledge of God, and bringing into captivity every thought to the obedience of Christ" (2 Corinthians 10:5) instead of looking on things "after the outward appearance . . . (2 Corinthians 10:7), but I was ignoring the Word of God in its entirety — a sure avenue to extinction.

It's a good thing George came bounding down the steps the next minute, hitting only every third one because he was so excited. If he hadn't shown up exactly when he did, my negative attitude might have talked me into irreversible corpsehood on a meat hook.

"Brother Hill, guess what!" he shouted. I wished he'd slow down, to conserve the oxygen in the place. I was feeling a little faint.

"Don't test me any more tonight, George," I whispered, panting for breath. *Is that what I said? Sounds out of character for a King's kid!* What was happening to me?

I did a quick check of my pulse. I was still alive, but just barely. I calculated how long it would take the local authorities to notify the next of kin when the inevitable happened. I wondered if my wife, Ruth, would remarry. I was imagining her at the undertaker's establishment, expressing her preference for the bronze casket, when George interrupted: "BrotherHill, I found a little attic window out over the roof—"

George was so glad, he was almost jumping up and down— delirium, I decided—and he seemed not to have noticed all the cobwebs lacing over his black suit. I noticed them, all right, and shuddered. The spiders that spit out those strings could have been black widows. If someone was bitten by a deadly poisonous spider and couldn't get out fast for medical attention, it'd be curtains for him in no time.

Do people dying from spider bites get rabid and attack innocent bystanders? I wondered. That *could* be worse than death by suffocation or a broken neck.

I inched away from George until my back hit the cold stone wall and sent more shivers through me. He didn't look rabid yet, but you could never tell. It would pay to stay out of reach.

With an awful foreboding, I knew the attic window would be barred and shuttered, like the windows downstairs, anyhow. Prisons never have any accidental exits.

"Don't try to get my hopes up, George," I warned him, keeping my distance. "The window is barred and shuttered. There's no stepladder, and if you think I'm going to jump out and add a broken neck to my spasmed ribs and squashed thumbs and disintegrated spinal disc—"

His eyes widened and mine probably did, too. Why, Jesus had given me a new spinal disc, years ago, and He'd taken care of my spasmed ribs and my squashed thumb—singular—in a perfectly satisfactory way. But as I heard my tongue magnifying my miseries, I felt pain all over my body, healed or not. My tongue was loose, a runaway, multiplying agony. It couldn't stop.

Again, readers who have learned how to live like King's kids will recognize that I was confirming the truth of a few more Scriptures:

> And the tongue is a fire, a world of iniquity: so is the tongue among our members, that it defileth the whole body, and setteth on fire the course of nature; and it is set on fire of hell. . . . the tongue can no man tame; it is an unruly evil, full of deadly poison.
>
> James 3:6, 8

My tongue was ministering hell, all right, and I was in the midst of it. Furthermore, I was proving that a man who has heard the Word, but doesn't do it, forgets what he looks like (James 1:23, 24). I'd even forgotten what I *was*! And, proving that the imaginations of a man's heart are only evil continually (Genesis 6:5), my mouth continued to spout poison: "I've been here in the Black Forest before," I hissed at George with the little voice I had left. "They roll up the sidewalks before eight o'clock. It'll be blacker than the inside of a cow's stomach, outside, and nobody will be within earshot for miles and miles. You can just find yourself another turkey, if we ever get out of here alive. . . ."

Maybe the Rapture would come in time. Or maybe it wouldn't. With my death-dealing attitude, I was hardly a candidate anyhow.

18

Return to the Word

I had reached bottom. My attitude insisted that my situation was utterly hopeless. There was nothing I could do. I hadn't anything to offer. I realized I was a poverty-stricken nobody. Unwittingly, by the grace of God, I was putting myself in the position recommended by the first be-attitude: "Blessed are the poor in spirit: for theirs is the kingdom of heaven" (Matthew 5:3).

"God, help me!" I moaned with my last breath and slumped to the floor, reckoning myself dead.

Amazingly, just as He had done twenty-five years before, on the day I first became a King's kid, God heard my cry and answered me, according to His promise:

> If my people, which are called by my name, shall humble themselves, and pray, and seek my face, and turn from their wicked ways; then will I hear from heaven, and will forgive their sin, and will heal their land.
>
> 2 Chronicles 7:14

He was already performing that Word, before I remembered it. George was *really* praising, and he advanced on me and shook my shoulders, hard, to get my attention. He was shouting at me: "Listen to what I'm trying to tell you, Brother Hill! I know how hopeless it *looks*. But King's kids don't go by appearances, remember? When I found that little window, it *wasn't* barred, and I stuck my head out to praise the Lord, like I thought you were doing down here in the vestibule—"

Was he accusing me? My ears were turning red. I couldn't remember another occasion when I'd turned my praiser off so completely, not since I'd become a King's kid. I'd heard some teachers recommend that, but I'd never followed along, knowing their teaching was not in line with God's Word.

What had happened to my attitude? And why?

I took a deep breath of the suddenly plentiful air—that window must have been bigger than I imagined—got to my feet, and began to thank God that George had been faithful to hang on to the presence of the Lord with praise even though I'd failed.

Naturally, I began to praise God for George and to thank Him that He hadn't left me locked in by myself, but had given me a witness who was also an intercessor.

"What happened when you stuck your neck out?" I asked, doing a complete about-face in my attitude, ready to hear the good news I knew was coming next. By the grace of God, I was a King's kid again, a winner in high victory after the temporary lapse that almost wiped me out.

"Well, I heard footsteps," he said, "so I hollered down, and somebody hollered back. I asked if Fritz was waiting out front to pick us up, and sure enough, he was. When Fritz came under the window, I told him our situation. He said he was glad to hear it, because seeing our car outside and the hotel all clammed up, he thought maybe the Rapture had come, and we'd gone to be with the Lord while he'd been left behind."

"Poor Fritz could have been having mixed emotions," I decided, wondering if his pity party had been as nearly fatal as mine. Couldn't have been, I concluded, because the way I'm built, I always overreact worse than anybody else. Then the Lord reminded me of what the Word says about mixed emotions: how the guy who has them is like a wave tossed by the sea, so he can't expect to receive anything from the Lord (James 1:6, 7). That set me off in new convulsions of counting joy and praising the Lord for the faithfulness and steadfastness and single-mindedness and perseverance He had planted in His servant George.

While I praised the Lord for George some more, George was praising the Lord that I was back in my right mind. Our combined praises were almost enough to take the roof off the building, but not quite. Anyhow, I couldn't feel locked in anymore, no matter how many keys were lost. I had hold of the real keys of the Kingdom right there, and they were the only keys I needed. Who cared whether or not we ever got out? The Lord was with us, and that was all that mattered. I could have rejoiced at staying locked up from then on, because I was so free in the Spirit, looking at the perfect law of liberty (James 1:23–25) because I was a hearer *and* a doer of the Word.

George's patience was being made perfect while I was entering new creaturehood again, and then he told me how he had thrown his car keys down to Fritz, so he could check to see if George had left the hotel-getting-out key in the car.

If I'd still been in my pity-party attitude, I'd have swallowed my gizzard on that one. I would have known the car keys would get lost in the dark, amongst all those cobblestones, and we'd not be able to move our vehicle even if we did get out of the hotel alive. But since I was back in praising gear, looking at the Lord instead of at the circumstances, I didn't even hold my breath when George told me about it. I just headed for the door, because I knew that what I had finally loosed on earth had already taken place in heaven, and all we had to do was to receive it. I knew we were captives who had been set free. I expected the door to open, and it did.

I learned the mechanics of the rest of it when Fritz explained how he had caught the keys—real bull's-eye—and knelt beside the car to ask the Lord where he should look for the hotel key. Somehow, after the prayer, he knew he was to look in the trunk. The big iron key was lying there on the carpet, just waiting to let us out.

When we arrived at the meeting, we were not surprised to find the Lord had used the slight delay in our appearing for real good. Not only had He given me a new testimony of how He is able to set the captives free—as long as there is one man of faith among them, one who stays in the right attitude toward God's Word—but He let the folks at the meeting use the extra time for a double-length preliminary song service to get the whole audience geared into praising the Lord with all their hearts. That made them able—in record numbers—to receive the other blessings the Lord had for them that night. Again, the tribulations the Lord allowed were better than no tribulations at all.

But how about the strange, unprecedented thing that had happened to me and my attitude when, to the natural man, the proceedings looked so dismal? Did the Lord have a use for that too? It was so grim being unable to praise the Lord. What was that all about?

19

Why Did It Happen?

or

Sweet Are the Uses of Unvictory

The Lord explained everything to me before I got up to speak, so I was able to share a brand-new lesson with the people.

"I didn't make King's kids to go it alone," His Spirit seemed to be saying to me. "I deliberately put them in fellowship with one another, so they can bear one another's burdens and pray for one another. I've had you in that position a lot in recent years, Hill, and you needed to see how it works when other folks are on the giving end of the stick. If George hadn't kept on praising, you'd have been a goner. But while you were brooding everything in sight into total disaster, he hung on to seeing the light at the end of the tunnel, based on his faith in the promises in My Word."

That was potent enough, but there was more. "Another thing, Hill. I wanted you to learn that you can never afford to boast about victory as if it were *your* doing—it's always by My grace—and I wanted you to know not to condemn the other guy when he can't

whoop it up. Pray for him; whoop it up *for* him, as George did for *you*.
That way, things are guaranteed to come out all right, and I'll get all
the glory. But when anybody forgets that grace to have right attitudes and grace to praise Me comes from Me, I have to teach him a
lesson."

"Yes, Lord." I was really hearing Him, but He rubbed it in a little
more, just to make sure I got the message.

"Next time," He said, "*you* might need to stand in the gap for
George, if *he* gets unhumble about these things. One of the reasons
King's kids can *know* I'm going to work every mess for good for them
is that you're not the only praiser out there. I still have thousands of
others who haven't bowed their knees to Baal" (1 Kings 19:18).

Baal—made me think of bellyaching. That's what I'd been
doing: complaining, griping, conjuring up fear. No wonder I had
gotten such miserable results. I had learned my lesson about boasting, all right. In addition to that, looking back on the whole adventure, I clearly realized how easy it is for someone who isn't praising
the Lord to brew up a whole witches' cauldron full of trouble—more
than he can handle—if he looks at circumstances instead of the Word
and lets his tongue magnify the problem instead of magnifying the
Lord.

There I had been, about to brood one little temporarily mis-
placed key into excruciating death by suffocation, starvation, lunatic
attack, rabies, and black-widow-spider bites, when there was no
possibility of any of those things happening; but they almost killed
me, anyhow. When my attitude was conditioned by the evidence of
my senses, I not only expected the worst the evidence could suggest,
but my mind made the situation more horrible, letting my sick head
create an army of boogeymen under every bed.

Whew! I was glad I was out of that one!

Thank God that King's kids don't have to misbehave the way I
did. They can avoid it by recognizing that they tend to fall into such
deception when they take their eyes off Him.

Count it all joy? Even temporary loss of praise? Of course! Even
that worked for good, so that this King's kid in training could share his
life with those about him.

Did it look good at the time? No way. It never does. But should we go by appearances? Does God? No. He made the whole world out of things that were invisible (Hebrews 11:3). If he'd been relying on appearances, regarding the evidence of His senses, we wouldn't even be here yet.

I've learned that to live like a King's kid, I can't afford to rely on the evidence of my senses, either. Instead, I expect God to pull the supernatural out of a hat whenever I need Him to do that.

Want another example? Read on.

20

Brunch, Anyone?

"Bear ye one another's burdens, and so fulfil the law of Christ," the Manufacturer tells us (Galatians 6:2). One morning in Germany, I really needed someone to do that for me.

A picture of perfect innocence, I had walked into a restaurant, looking for something to eat. Little did I know it was going to spell trouble.

Since I couldn't read the menu, and my German gastronomic vocabulary was limited to *Brot, Käse,* and *Kaffee* (bread, cheese, and coffee), that's what I ordered. The little waitress seemed to understand, and that's what she brought me. It was good, too, and when I had eaten every crumb and drained the last drop from my mug, the waitress came back and handed me my check.

I couldn't read a word of it, and I didn't try, just took an American five-dollar bill from my pocket and laid it on the table. I hadn't yet changed my American dollars to German marks, but I trusted a five-spot should be adequate to cover a midmorning snack, with some change left over for a tip.

I didn't know I was in for it, but I soon found out. When the fraulein approached my table and saw that five-dollar bill, she reacted as if she had confronted a two-headed reticulated python. She backed up against the farthest wall of the cafe and began to rocket mouth at me in the most voluble German I'd ever encountered. As if that weren't enough, she soon summoned a middle-sized waitress, and the two of them let me have it with both barrels.

I just sat there praising the Lord, of course, knowing I *hadn't* committed the unpardonable sin, even though they acted as if I had. Soon there were three waitresses ranged against the flowered wallpaper, all of them mad. I was reminded of the papa bear, mama bear, and little baby bear in the nursery tale, and they were laying it on me so heavily that if there had been an open window, I'd have made like Goldilocks and split.

Not having that alternative, I stayed put, continuing to praise the Lord and sending up an SOS to heaven: "Lord, it looks as if I could use a few reinforcements here. I'm about to be outnumbered. Could You spare an angel for a few minutes?"

I was basing my prayer on a couple of Scriptures, one in Hebrews, the other in Psalms: "Are not all angels ministering spirits sent to serve those who will inherit salvation?" (Hebrews 1:14 NIV). "Then they cried unto the Lord in their trouble, and he delivered them out of their distresses" (Psalms 107:6).

I was in distress, all right. I needed angels, or *something*, even before the three waitresses left and came back with the manager, who joined them in a quartet of sermonizing at me. If I hadn't known to praise the Lord, it would have been awful, especially when they all turned their eyes in unison out the window toward the big, brick building across the street with heavy steel bars across every opening.

It didn't take a genius to figure out they were thinking in terms of consigning me to the local jailhouse.

My prayer life improved 100 percent. "Lord, You've got a problem. I'm glad it's not my problem. I've come over here to brag on You

in twenty-four places in the next two weeks in Germany, Switzerland, and Austria. Lord, if I'm locked up in the jailhouse, I can't
preach to anybody except to those in the pokey with me—rather
limited numbers, unless they're having a crime wave. But it's all right
with me, Lord. Whatever You want, I'm willing."

By the time I'd finished my prayer, I was equally ready for
hoosegow or heaven, not sure I'd be able to tell the difference,
because when a King's kid is praising the King, one place is as
heavenly as the next one.

Being so at liberty in my spirit, I wasn't bothered by what I could
see and hear—the increasing anger of the manager and his three
bears—just curious about how the Lord was going to work it all out. I
didn't even feel guilty that my laying the five-spot on the table
seemed to have canceled every peace treaty between our nation and
theirs for the last 700 years. Jesus was in full charge.

When I asked Him what I should do next, the Word came,
"Having done all, stand and see the salvation of the Lord" (*see*
Ephesians 6:13; Exodus 14:13). That put me on notice that I was on
the right track in refusing to succumb to the common-sense conclusion
that I was in for disaster, but to watch for the Lord's still invisible,
inaudible salvation.

Just then a distinguished-looking gentleman walked in the door
and approached my table. I knew he was a special emissary sent to
help me out.

"I say, old chap, you appear to be having trouble," he said,
speaking perfect English with an Oxford accent above the clamor of
the shouting, discordant quartet in the corner. I didn't argue with
him; I just let the situation speak for itself.

"May I help you?" he asked me next.

"Any help would be welcomed at this point," I told him, explain-
ing that my innocent act in putting American greenery on the table
had sent the frauleins and their manager into a rage.

He nodded knowingly, picked up my check and the green two-
headed python, walked over to the manager, bowed, spoke a few

words that sounded German, and instantly there was a complete change of atmosphere in the restaurant. It was beautiful.

The manager came over to my table and bowed to me. The big waitress bowed, the middle waitress bowed, and the little waitress gave a curtsey. All four of them kept genuflecting in my direction until I felt like visiting royalty. Apparently the old gentleman was acquainted with the exchange rate between marks and dollars, because he put a certain amount of change on my table while the other four were still doing their waist-slimming exercises.

Overwhelmed with the calm after the storm, I turned to thank the old gentleman who had obviously been God's instrument for saving me from a drafty night in a dungeon. But he wasn't there. He wasn't anywhere. That's when I suspected that a money-changing angel had been sent to my assistance.

Another Scripture had been fulfilled in the midst of things. It came at me full force as I got up to leave, continuing to praise the Lord: "When a man's ways please the Lord, he maketh even his enemies to be at peace with him" (Proverbs 16:7).

We are always pleasing God when we are praising Him with an attitude that His Word is true. It's good to know that. It's even better to do it. that's what living the Bible is all about. And He was about to prove it one more time.

21

A Room at the Inn

Soon after the money-changing angel came to my rescue in the nick of time, other special arrangements were made for my comfort when circumstances seemed less than perfect at the outset. This further demonstration of God's ability to supply all the needs of King's kids according to His riches in glory (Philippians 4:19) happened in Munich, where I was scheduled to speak at a FGBMFI convention.

The first thing I learned at 6:00 P.M. when I arrived travel grimy and saddle weary at the big hotel where the meeting was to be held, was that there was no room for me at the inn. Somebody had goofed and failed to make a reservation for me, and since there were several conventions in progress in the city, the waiting list was long.

Of course my name was put at the very bottom of the list. In the natural, there would never be enough cancellations for me to be entitled to a mattress unless there was a major earthquake, wiping out half the population while it preserved all the pallets.

The situation didn't look very promising; it didn't feel very promising. Every evidence collected by my senses said, "Too bad, Hill. Looks like you're in for a night of curling up in the car or stretching out under a couch in the lobby." I could see the tops of couches were already claimed.

But being full of promises of God, my attitude couldn't be discouraged. I knew something wonderful was going to happen because I'd put Him in charge of my day—and my night.

Relying on His Word, I knew He was going to work all things together for good, even the fact of my nonexistent reservations. I knew, further, that He was going to supply all my needs, and that He wouldn't dream of forsaking me. With promises like that from a God who cannot lie, a fellow would be an idiot to get a gloomy attitude by looking at circumstances.

So I stood there, expectant as a lit firecracker on the Fourth of July. I knew that something would go off in the fullness of time, which could be any minute now.

While I waited, I listened to the pagans pouting in the lobby, griping about their nonexistent reservations while I praised the Lord for mine. I could see that the poor desk clerk wanted to pacify everybody, but it was humanly impossible.

How can a fellow get preferential King's-kid treatment in a case like that? Certainly not by the usual human methods. They *can't* work when that's what everybody else is relying on. I was glad to have something so much better on my side. So I just got as comfortable as I could and praised Jesus for what He was working out for me while I waited on the Lord.

I knew He had been with me as I had driven up through the country from way down in Switzerland that day, so He was aware that I needed a shower and a place to get horizontal for a little rejuvenation before the banquet started at 7:30. All I had to do to get special treatment was to put myself in the hands of the King. He would treat me like a King's kid if I would do my part and act like one.

How does a King's kid act? Why, he's always praising the King of course, staying in glory no matter what is going on around him. I started to get on with it, to get myself securely hooked to His wavelength.

"No room at the inn!" I crowed. "Hallelujah! That puts me in good company, Lord, because that's the way they treated You, too. Praise the Lord!

"Lord, I can see this is going to be a very fancy banquet, in this brand-new hotel and all. Everybody else is going to be all spiffed up, deodorized, and decked out in their glad rags. But if You want me at the head table in my grubby corduroy jacket with patches on the elbows, B.O. under my arms, and tater rows round my neck, I'm going to praise You for it. On the other hand, if You want to find a place for me to shower and shave and put on my clean shirt and my Sunday suit, I'll be glad to praise You for that, instead.

"Doesn't matter one way or the other to me, Lord, not a particle. Just so You're satisfied.

"Later on, I think it would be nice to have a bed for the night, but if sleeping in the lobby or curling up in the car suits You better, it sounds perfect to me, Lord. I'm glad I have nothing to offer, that You're the One in charge. Just have Your way, Lord."

If anybody had been listening to me praise Jesus for the state in which I found myself, he might have thought I sounded stupid. But what I was doing was guaranteed to work. I had the Manufacturer's Word for it, and I was brooding on the irrevocable promise in Matthew 16:19 (NIV) again: "I will give you the keys of the kingdom of heaven; whatever you bind on earth will be bound in heaven, and whatever you loose on earth will be loosed in heaven."

Having met the conditions by loosing any anxiety about the situation, putting it all in His hands, I knew He could act to get His will done on earth as it was already done in heaven. Whatever His will was, it was bound to be better than anything I could ever dream up. Waiting expectantly for His will to manifest itself was kind of exciting.

Believe it or not, just a few minutes after He had given me the no-room "good news," the desk clerk came out from behind the desk, threaded his way through the clamoring, complaining pagans, and singled me out for VIP attention.

"Herr Hugel," he said—that's German for Mister Hill—"I'm sorry you've been inconvenienced, but I can now offer you a place to shower and change and a temporary bed for a little rest before your banquet. That's all I can give you at the moment, but—"

"No need to apologize," I told him. "That's all I can use at the moment, praise the Lord. A place to shower and change and a bed for a little horizontal before the vertical—that's perfect. Couldn't use anything else. If I had a bed for the night already, it would just be in the way. I can't possibly need one until midnight or so."

A fine young bellhop showed me to the swimming pool area, where I had my choice of rooms for a shower, another cubicle for changing my clothes, and a Red Cross Emergency Room that had no patients or staff at the moment, just a nice, white, empty bed made up for me—perfect for a catnap.

While pagans kept complaining that they didn't have one room, I was luxuriating with three rooms at my exclusive disposal.

At seven-thirty, I showed up at the banquet table, sparkling clean, dressed in my best, and well rested, ready to feast and then do my favorite thing: brag on Jesus.

Furthermore, before I got up to speak, a messenger approached the head table and handed me the key to what turned out to be one of the best rooms in the establishment.

Where had the room come from? Why was it made available to me? I didn't ask questions; I just thanked Jesus that He knew all the answers.

Did an ahead-of-time attitude of victory have anything to do with changing the circumstances in my case from nadir to zenith—the lowest to the highest? with zooming me from the last place to the top priority? Search me.

All I know is that after the banquet, when I headed for my room, key in hand, the lobby was still spilling over with wrinkled, grubby grumblers with five o'clock shadows, whose names had been ahead of mine on the waiting list.

You figure it out. Better yet, conduct an experiment. The next time you find yourself in a less-than-the-best position, try the world's way of getting out of it. If it works, let me know. The King's-kid way works so well for me, I can't usually talk myself into trying the world's way anymore—not after that German castle episode. But then, I don't try too hard, since brooding on heaven's best guarantees—and gets—such superperfect results.

Living the Bible. Try it for heaven on earth.

22

How About Hard Cases?

"But does this brooding on the best, praising the Lord in *all* things, work for really *serious*, important problems for other people?" I hear someone squawking. And while I listen, they go into orbit, detailing the miseries of Great-aunt Lizzie, practically an invalid, whose husband eloped with the milkman, leaving her as the sole support of a dozen young'uns, all of them triplets under five years old.

Well, I have to admit I've never been in exactly *that* situation — and I doubt that Aunt Lizzie has either — but I've had some close calls of my own (you can read about my three fatal heart attacks in *How to Be a Winner*), and I've had opportunity to observe closely and to hear about far more. In every case, where the sufferer came to the point of recognizing and rejoicing in his own inability — and God's ability — to handle the situation, and where he began to stay in an attitude of praise and thanksgiving toward God, brooding on the truth of His Word, the situation opened up, hatching out good for the brooder and glory for God.

It can't happen any other way.

Let me tell you just a few case histories in the lives of other people, changing names and places in some cases to keep the brooders anonymous, but clewing you in on the essential fact situation.

One of the most amazing cases that has ever come to my personal attention involved a young Canadian woman, Kay Golbeck (and that's her real name), who almost half a century ago came down with what had to be the world's worst case of every kind of arthritis you can name. For eight and a half years she lay in Saint Joseph's Hospital in Toronto, Canada, brooding on the promises of God found in the Manufacturer's Handbook in the letter of James:

> Is any sick among you? let him call for the elders of the church; and let them pray over him, anointing him with oil in the name of the Lord: And the prayer of faith shall save the sick, and the Lord shall raise him up; and if he have committed sins, they shall be forgiven him.
>
> James 5:14, 15

When Kay's mind had been so conformed to the mind of Christ that she knew that Scripture, like all the others she had tried, just *had* to be true, she did the Word and experienced the results. She called for the elders of the church, was prayed over, was anointed with oil, and fell into a deep sleep. The next morning, even though she hadn't been able to move a single part of her body for over two years, and although common sense would have said, "Ridiculous! That'll never work in your case; you're too far gone!" Kay Golbeck got out of bed and walked. A real miracle!

A little over a year later, she began the first year of an eight-year stretch in a very demanding position as chaplain in a penitentiary for women at Goochland, Virginia. The last I heard, Kay was doing the cooking and serving of meals—hardly a job for an invalid—to dozens of people at Singing Waters, the internationally known retreat center the Lord had her establish at Orangeville, Canada, years ago when she seemed to be dying again—with myasthenia gravis, this time. But she kept her attitude in line with God's Word, and He delivered her once more.

You can read part of Kay's mind-blowing true story in her book, *Lord, How Will You Get Me Out of This Mess?* (Chosen Books, Lincoln, Virginia). The title asks a pretty good question, eh? Whatever mess you're in, He can get you out of it somehow if you'll be obedient to read His Word, brood on it day and night, believe on it, and then *do* it. Nothing is too hard for God!

A teenager of my acquaintance—call her Katie—was growing up determined to have her own way in everything if it killed her. Not surprisingly, with that kind of attitude, she almost landed among the tombstones as a permanent resident.

The trouble probably all started when Katie's mother and father decided that the only way they could live happily ever after was if they never saw each other again—ever. The divorce proceedings were long and hairy, and the fracas over custody of the kid left poor Katie feeling as if she had been shredded, grated, pulled apart, compressed in the garbage compactor, and stomped on by all the hostile festivities. When everything was settled, Katie decided to get as far away from both parents as was humanly possible. Apollo was already manned, so she settled for continuing her education on the other side of the Atlantic, where nobody could tell her what to do.

Ironically enough, Katie landed smack in the middle of a British boarding school that was so tightly regimented the students even *breathed* in unison. Katie liked the academics, though, so instead of dropping out and heading for home, she informed her dad that she had to have her own car and her own apartment while she pursued her studies at her own pace. When he declined to furnish the green stuff for that life-style, she made up her mind to starve herself to death to get what she wanted. How that was supposed to work, I don't know, but her mind had it all figured out.

When the school authorities noticed that Katie was getting pale around the gills from undernourishment, they stood over her and insisted that she clean her plate. She did it, and then excused herself immediately thereafter to go to the ladies' room to brush her teeth. She had a mouthful of braces, of course, like every well-endowed teenager, and after-meal brushing was highly recommended by the orthodontist. Out of sight and earshot, she ran the handle end of her toothbrush past her tonsillectomy scars until she triggered a stomach-emptying response.

The school authorities couldn't understand why she kept on losing weight when she ate so heartily at their insistence. If they'd read their history books, they'd have found a clue. The old saying, "What goes up must come down," was reversed in the vomitoriums of the ancient Roman Empire to read, "What goes down must come up."

When Katie's condition worsened to the point where the head-master of the school feared that the next jet stream from a passing carrier pigeon might blow her away forever, he put her on a plane back to the United States. There she was hospitalized with anorexia nervosa, a serious ailment in which a patient who has been skinnying down to a sliver on purpose *can* reach the point of fatal irreversibility.

It almost happened to my friend Katie. Six feet tall, she fell to ninety pounds and looked more like the inside of a toothpick than a human being. For a while, it appeared that invisibility was just around the corner.

Fortunately, Katie's grandma, a King's kid from way back, came to the rescue just in time, got on her prayer bones, praised the Lord for the situation just as it was, *knowing* God was going to work it for good, according to His promise. Sure enough, He did.

Katie started to eat again, got out of the hospital, and founded a chapter of Anorexics Anonymous in her own town to help others as bad off as she had been. Today Katie is back in school—university level—and is more interested in seeing the Lord have *His* way than in getting her own.

Some more examples?

I know a pastor who was asked to leave his church because he had received the baptism in the Holy Ghost, and people were getting healed when he laid hands on them. He and his wife had nowhere to live except in their *car* for months, but they kept praising the Lord the whole time, knowing He was going to work it for good for them. The result? Not only did they get a job pastoring another church, the congregation loved them so much they deeded the parsonage to them and said they could live there forever, rent free, whether the man preached or not. The congregation covenanted that for the rest of the couple's lives, they would take care of all maintenance on the house and keep them furnished with a new car.

I heard about a deacon whose daughter, without benefit of clergy, had moved in with a boy who wasn't even saved. In the natural, the father hated the situation, but he decided to do the Bible thing: to *know* that God was working it for good for him. Sure enough, his daughter and the young man both sold out to Jesus, were filled with the Holy Ghost, got married, went to Bible School, and are now serving as missionaries in South America.

I know a woman—call her Trixie—who grew up on the wrong side of everything. Her stepmother hated her with a purple passion; her father sided with the stepmother; and life was full speed downhill all the way. When Trixie married the first man who asked her, just to escape from home, divorce was just around the corner. After the marriage hit the skids, Trixie was left with a well-established alcoholic habit and a couple of kids to raise with no visible support from their father.

Sound terrible? It was. But somebody, somewhere, was praying for Trixie. She met Jesus, and He changed her attitude from one of resentment and being sorry for herself to one of rejoicing and being glad for Him and the truth of His Word. Once her attitude changed, the gal who couldn't cope with anything became victorious in the most unvictory-looking circumstances imaginable.

One day she got a phone call from a faraway state where her son had been living with a succession of floozies in a progression of flophouses, each one more cockroachy than the last. The voice on the other end of the line identified herself as Becky, said she was sixteen, pregnant, and that her live-in lover boy, Trixie's son, was in the pokey and needed 600 smackers for bail-out money.

Could you praise the Lord in the midst of a mess such as that? Could you have an attitude that rejoiced that God would work it for good?

Trixie's bank account said zero, but her mouth shouted, "Glory! Lord, make him so miserable he can't live without You!" She sat down and wrote her son a letter, included in it a sinner's prayer, and sent it off—without a check. Afterward she acknowledged that she could do nothing, but that God could do everything if she trusted in Him. And she thanked Him for everything, exactly as it was.

How do these things work? Don't ask me. I just know that they work. And I like to be on the receiving end.

Trixie was counting on God to do everything, according to His Word, above all she could ask or think or even believe. And it happened. Locked in his cell, with a murderer on the bunk above him and a man convicted of armed robbery on the bunk below, Trixie's son got on his knees and prayed the sinner's prayer and asked Jesus to take over his messed-up life. Today he is gainfully employed, married to Becky in holy matrimony, the baby is the apple of Grandma Trixie's eye, and the house where the young folks live is a place where folks can go to meet the Lord. Can you beat that? Want to hear another?

One of my good friends is a judge in North Carolina. One day he became suddenly ill while he was seated at the bench and had to be helped from the courtroom. There followed days in bed and tests and more tests. Symptoms—acute dizziness and hearing loss—and X rays led to a tough diagnosis: acute labyrinthitis and a tumor on the eighth cranial nerve. The tumor had to go. Even a healthy tumor growing inside a healthy cranium makes things too crowded for comfort.

Surgery was scheduled, business engagements canceled, arrangements made for someone else to hold court during an anticipated four-month recovery period. The judge told his wife what minister he wanted to preach his graduation-to-glory funeral sermon in case the fullness of his time was up. Nobody shed any tears, because everyone knew Jesus would supply every need, no matter what was required. The perfect peace that bypasses all human understanding was in motion.

Meanwhile, the judge, his family, and the rest of the saints near and far were praying for healing; and they were praising the Lord for His Word, which guaranteed He'd work it all for good, whether it looked like it or not.

On the day before surgery, one final test was run to guide the neurosurgeons in how to proceed the next day. Result? Bafflement and glory!

No tumor! No surgery! No sick leave with pay! No funeral!

The judge went back to work, praising God for a new testimony of His power and His love. The judge is still deaf in his left ear from the attack, but he's brooding on the Word where Jesus says, ". . . the deaf hear . . ." (Luke 7:22), knowing it will hatch out in whatever the fullness of time happens to be in this particular case. In the meantime, his grace is sufficient.

"But you're always talking victory!" kibitzers complain. "What if it doesn't turn out that way? What if Kay Golbeck hadn't recovered? What if Katie hadn't gotten well? What if the judge's tumor hadn't disappeared? What if he'd had surgery, and the thing was malignant, and the doctors couldn't get it all? What if . . .?"

You're free to brood up a negative attitude like that if you choose, but it's not for me. God says I'm to think on the things that are lovely and of good report. If the "what ifs" happen—and even King's kids have been known to die when God says their time on earth is up—hallelujah! Leaving this place, in God's fullness of time for them, they enter a better place, where we'll all have a grand reunion some day at another level of eternal life in Jesus.

We could debate the "what ifs" and recite case histories until we're dead with old age, but no argument or case history will persuade you better than your own testimony when you begin to brood on the promises of God in your own total-disaster situation and see Him do His thing in the midst of the atmosphere of praise you create, the atmosphere in which God dwells, when you get your attitude in agreement with the Word of God.

"But how can I *know* it will work for me?" There's only one way: Try it.

For an easy-to-consult alphabetical guide to Scriptures for brooding up superperfect results in the case of:

Lawsuits

Husband-Wife Haggles

Fear

Firebombs

Depression

Anxiety

Heart Trouble

Boob-tube-itis

Overeating

Ignorance

Anger

Impatience

and anything else that ails you, consult my *Instant Answers for King's Kids in Training*. It's packed with promises from the God who can't lie, just waiting for you to brood them into reality in your own life.

Happy brooding!